God Promised Me Wings to Fly

PRAISE FOR
GOD PROMISED ME WINGS TO FLY

Tragedy . . . *redeemed*? When we are in the depths of pain, we can hardly imagine how we will get through it. To think that we can actually survive, and then use our struggles to offer a lifeline to others, isn't even a possibility.

But Janet Grillo shows us that it is. In this deeply moving and vulnerable, yet hope-filled memoir, Janet takes us on a journey through discovering her husband's death by suicide and his secret life, battling her own thoughts of suicide, and ultimately finding healing, self-realization, and faith.

She shows us that grief is something to embrace, and that grief can actually offer us a path toward a powerful purpose in life—one of using the pain to make a difference in the lives of others.

Vicki Huber-Rudawsky
Two-time Olympic athlete

God Promised Me Wings to Fly is a heartfelt expression of the many traumas Janet Grillo has faced. She writes from her heart and shares with the reader how her Christian beliefs helped her survive and overcome extremely challenging times. Janet's kindness and obvious care of others shine through the pages. You will enjoy this book, as it will motivate you to move forward with hopefulness for your own future.

Carole Fawcett
Writer and editor

You never know when you're going to meet someone who will change the way you think. Janet did that for me. She shows there is always hope. To see the person is real, then to hear her story and how she powered through so much gives hope for all of us who understand that life isn't comfortable, and it's up to us to keep moving forward using our wings to fly.

Rick DeDonato
Marketing professional; author, Pipsie Nature Detective Series

Janet Grillo's honest, vulnerable, raw, and inspiring recounting of her life's journey will give hope no matter what devastating betrayal you face or financial adversity you must overcome. Read and discover that you too can find the courage, determination, and self-love to honor and value who you are despite your circumstances, because God always has your back and will give you *wings to fly.*

Marty L. Ward
Transformation strategist

When I first picked up Janet's book, as with all books of a religious bent, I was skeptical. How would this author differ from the crowds of others who simply say *look to God* devoid of details or rational counsel? Her book immediately drew me in. She deserves high praise for merely surviving. But more than that, she moved forward to create an empathetic and educational tool, replete with wisdom and great advice. There's something very different about this book. It doesn't insist that I believe this way or that, but instead, it empowers with inspiring insights. I gladly recommend this book to anyone seeking guidance through the most severe of trauma.

Howard F. Bronson
Author, How to Heal a Broken Heart in 30 Days

In *God Promised Me Wings to Fly*, Janet Grillo spoke directly to me! When I lost my spouse suddenly, I thought the world, as I knew it, had stopped, but it just took a pause. When Janet wrote, "There is no way that God would make me go through so much pain without having something wonderful on the other side," I smiled and said, "Yes . . . that's the truth!"

Janet stands as a witness to death, family turmoil, depression, and many of life's damaging and ugly moments. More importantly, she stands as a witness to faith, hope, love, and many of life's good moments.

Debby Montgomery Johnson
Founder, The Woman Behind the Smile, Inc.;
best-selling author; speaker; victim advocate

It is rare to stumble across something that touches your life that is a real game-changer. That is precisely what *God Promised Me Wings to Fly* did for me. I recommend this book to anyone that has ever experienced or witnessed tragedy and heartbreak.

Janet Grillo's story is an agonizing and ultimately redemptive tale of a woman mentally crushed after her allegedly Mafia-connected husband's untimely but questionable suicide. She was left alone to deal with all the questions and suspicions. With nothing but fear and anxiety, Janet spiraled into an abyss of depression and despair. Her tale is dark, but through faith and writing letters to God, Janet survived the tragedy and heartbreak. The reader will truly comprehend the power of faith, empathize with the horror she suffered, and recognize the healing powers of God.

Benjamin Higgs
Author; CEO, Start Marketing Inc.

JANET V. GRILLO

GOD
PROMISED ME
WINGS TO FLY

Life for Survivors After Suicide

NEW YORK

LONDON • NASHVILLE • MELBOURNE • VANCOUVER

God Promised Me Wings to Fly

Life for Survivors After Suicide

Published in New York, New York, by Morgan James Publishing. Morgan James is a trademark of Morgan James, LLC. www.MorganJamesPublishing.com

A **FREE** ebook edition is available for you
or a friend with the purchase of this print book.

CLEARLY SIGN YOUR NAME ABOVE

Instructions to claim your free ebook edition:
1. Visit MorganJamesBOGO.com
2. Sign your name CLEARLY in the space above
3. Complete the form and submit a photo
   of this entire page
4. You or your friend can download the ebook
   to your preferred device

ISBN 9781631953620 paperback
ISBN 9781631953637 eBook
Library of Congress Control Number:
2020948156

Cover Design by:
Judy Bullard, Custom Book Covers
customebookcovers.com

Interior Design by:
Christopher Kirk
www.GFSstudio.com

Morgan James is a proud partner of Habitat for Humanity Peninsula
and Greater Williamsburg. Partners in building since 2006.

Get involved today! Visit
MorganJamesPublishing.com/giving-back

In God's silent words He promised me wings to fly.
Come hell or high water, I am going to hold Him to His promise.
—Janet V. Grillo

CONTENTS

ACKNOWLEDGMENTS

When I sat down to make a list of the people I was grateful for and who supported me after my husband's tragic death, I immediately thought about my family. Foremost, I thought about my daughter, Amy, and my granddaughter, Mackenzie.

Amy immediately came to my aid, later gave me the space I needed to work on myself, and toward the end of my time living with her and her family, gave me tough love to encourage me to believe in myself and stand on my own two feet. Today, I am in a perfect place, and I can thank my daughter for that.

Mackenzie was only six-months-old when my husband died. My daughter brought her around as much as possible. I witnessed Mackenzie's struggle with feeding herself, standing, and walking on her own. I related to the struggles she was facing, because I was struggling with the same. Unbeknownst to Mackenzie, she was my muse and inspiration—a constant reminder that life is worth living and I should never give up on myself.

My family was incredibly supportive in the early years after Tony's death. They were not only there when I needed them most, they surprised me many times to bring joy into my life, especially when I had to face the first holidays and anniversaries without my husband.

God was the most important One in my life before, during, and after my husband's tragic death and the circumstances surrounding it. I did not mention Him first here, because I honestly could not imagine a living God who would allow someone to go through so much pain. Although I cried out to God on many occasions, I felt my cry for help fell on deaf ears. I know that God saw me struggle and saw me question His existence, yet He never abandoned me and chose to introduce His presence and miracles into my life one baby step at a time.

I learned to wait on God's timing. I knew that when I kept God in the forefront of my life, life was more comfortable and less stressful. My thirst for God and God's Word grows stronger each day. God helped me rise from a fetal position, thinking of myself as a victim, to a victorious woman seeking ways to make a difference in others' lives.

Terry Whalin, an author in his own right, is also my acquisition manager at Morgan James Publishing Company. I met Terry through a God connection. Someone I met as an acquaintance contacted me and requested an interview for their podcast. At the end of our interview, she mentioned that she was thinking about writing a book and that Terry Whalin was her friend.

She gave me Terry's contact information. Since I had already self-published *God Promised Me Wings to Fly*, I asked Terry if he would read my second book, *My Victory Journal*, to see if it had any substance. I did not want to spend hundreds of hours editing it if it was not worth publishing. Terry asked me to send him a copy of both books. He forwarded them to Wes Taylor, acquisition manager for the faith division of Morgan James. Two weeks later, Terry called and offered me two book contracting deals. I accepted, and Terry gave me the name of Ginger Kolbaba. I hired Ginger as my editor for this book and all future books.

In one of the letters I received from God, He told me that He would put the right people into my life to help make my book a great success. I genuinely believe that Ginger was a godsend.

Before working with Ginger, I thought of myself as a good writer. During and after working with her, I found myself becoming a great writer. I still have much to learn. Ginger is a fantastic editor and teacher. Every day, I strive to be a better student. Because of her expertise in polishing my writing, this book will touch many hearts.

In my eyes, Monsignor Lemon from Immaculate Heart of Mary (IHM) in Wilmington, Delaware, was my closest physical connection to God. His suggestion to take RCIA (Rite of Christian Initiation of Adults) classes was an excellent suggestion to get to know God better and to considerer becoming a Catholic. Whenever I approached Monsignor Lemon with a question, he always responded with the question, "What does your heart tell you to do?" I searched my heart and always found the right answer.

Rick DeDonato is well-known in Wilmington, Delaware, as a great marketing agent. I met with Rick after I self-published my first book, *My Secret Journal*. Rick told me that my book was good, but not great. Once I told him my back story, he suggested that I rewrite it to share my story of *Victim to Victory*. He took me to a place where I did not want to go. To write my story, I had to relive it. Today, thanks in part to him, I am an influential person with a desire to help others heal after a tragedy. Rick was a godsend. I will forever be grateful to him.

I met Marty L. Ward at a Woman of Excellence meeting in Melbourne, Florida. She approached me because of my sallow demeanor and because I was not mingling with the other women there. She took a hands-on approach and stuck her finger in my back, encouraging me to stand tall. Marty knew that I was suffering from something emotional and offered to help.

I met with Marty, and we discussed the antagonist in my life, including my husband's death and the circumstances around it. She pointed out that I should view the tragedies in my life as gifts, and one day I will use my experiences to help people. Because of Marty's expertise in helping others, I acquired her as a board member for my nonprofit Journey of Hope Survivors, Inc. Marty, thank you for your wisdom and friendship.

I have never met Rhonda Byrne, author of *The Secret,* however, I wish to acknowledge her here. I used *The Secret*'s teaching to never let go of the power of my dreams. Reading her book and applying the Law of Attraction to my life helped me become the person I am today. Because Rhonda influenced my life, I became a writer.

I have also never met Tony Robbins, but when I do, I will thank him personally for saving my life. After my husband's tragic death, I found myself in a fetal position. I truly believe that God selected the television channel in the wee hours of the morning to introduce me to the *Anthony Robbins 30-Day Personal Power Program for Unlimited Success.* Even though I had challenges committing to anything to improve my mental-health quality, I committed to the thirty-day challenge. The baby-step approach forever changed my life.

I never heard of Joyce Meyer until she spoke to me through my television in the wee hours of the morning. I could not sleep after spending the entire day and night in a fetal position. I heard a loud voice talking directly to me. "Why are you laying there feeling sorry for yourself. You are the only one responsible for your happiness." Joyce was my first wake-up call to get up and get moving. I read many Joyce Meyer books and even had the opportunity to attend a Joyce Meyer event in Hershey, PA.

I read John Maxwell's book Failing Forward: Turning Mistakes into Stepping Stones for Success at least ten times and carried it around like a Bible. This book helped me understand that failing is part of the process of succeeding. This book gave me hope to never give up on my dreams. Thank you, John.

Judy Bullard is the owner of Custom ebook Covers. I found Judy while searching on the internet looking for a cover designer for my book. I looked at more than two thousand photos before I found the image of the little girl held aloft. Judy performed great magic with the picture and created a magical cover. Thank you, Judy.

I met Vicki Huber-Rudawsky through my daughter, Amy. Both are runners. Vicki is a twice Olympian who is well known for her running accomplishments and making a difference in many people's lives. She is a humble and very approachable person. I had the opportunity to experience Vicki's kindness and giving during a race in Wilmington. I wrote about the race in the last chapter of this book. Thank you, Vicki, for making a difference in people's lives, especially children.

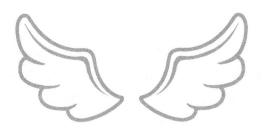

CHAPTER 1

A NIGHT TO REMEMBER

Suicide
The word caught your attention, didn't it? The truth is, suicide catches everyone's
attention. It's the actions leading up to suicide that go unnoticed.
—Author Unknown

M y husband's demeanor had been distant for the past few weeks. Whenever I asked him what was wrong, he'd only tell me, "Work has been very stressful."

Tony was the president of his family's business, Quality Automotive Parts, which his father established in 1961. The company specialized in selling used automotive parts to rebuilders. Tony's father did not give Tony a choice about working for the company, so whatever dreams Tony had about his future dissolved when he started there. In 1980s, Tony's father had an accident that caused him to retire. Because Tony was the oldest son, he inherited the title of president. He worked hard and long hours to succeed and make his father proud, as he managed more than one hundred accounts nationally and internationally. Along with endless meetings, stress appeared on the agenda every workday.

And I worried about him. Because of the more intense stress he seemed to be under for the past weeks, I wanted to do something special for him. On the morning of December 12, 2001, I awoke with a goal: to prepare a romantic dinner for two.

That will take Tony's mind off of his work, I thought.

I went to the store and purchased all the ingredients I needed to make his favorite dish—his Italian mother's spaghetti and meatballs. Though I was not a very good cook, I had worked hard to master that dish. The sauce ("gravy," to many Italians) has to cook many hours to release the hot sausage and meatball flavors. Of all the dishes that my mother-in-law cooked, this was her family's favorite. Her grandchildren called her "Mom-Mom Meatball."

After I mixed together all the ingredients, I set it on the stove to cook, and turned my attention to setting the table. As the hours passed, the smell of Italy filled the air, growing my anticipation for having a wonderful evening with my husband.

I set the table with china and crystal and placed candles to create a romantic atmosphere. I even bought a large bouquet of flowers. Everything was in place, including a red linen tablecloth and napkins.

Stepping back from the table, I smiled at my work. *He's going to be so thrilled.*

Around 4:00 p.m., Tony called. "Hello, darling. I thought it would be nice to have a romantic dinner tonight at Piccolina Toscana."

Though Piccolina Toscana was one of our favorite restaurants, I felt disappointed. *I just spent the entire day shopping, cooking, and creating the perfect setting for a romantic dinner for two.* My irritation at this change of plans got the best of my tone. "That sounds great, however, I thought we could eat at home tonight. I already started cooking dinner."

"Let's plan to eat your meal this weekend," he said. "We can invite friends to join us."

Although I was disappointed with his insistence, not to mention all the work I'd put into creating the perfect dining experience, I agreed.

I went into the kitchen and turned the heat off on the stove. I did not know why it was so important to Tony to take me out to dinner. But it was a nice gesture.

Maybe he realized how much stress he is under and wants to do for me what I wanted to do for him, I thought, a smile coming to my face. If that was the case, I would look my best for him. I refreshed my make-up and chose an outfit that Tony had purchased for me a little while back.

One thing that always made me smile was when Tony and I dressed to perfection when we went out to dinner. Tony always presented himself as being very successful and insisted that my appearance look the same.

My work in the jewelry industry had its perks. I accented each outfit with gold and diamonds. People often commented on the quality of Tony's ties, and as crazy as it seemed, men would ask him how much his ties cost. He always gave the same answer: "This tie cost more than your house." And everyone would laugh. Tony had the reputation of wanting to be a stand-up comedian. He always enjoyed making people laugh. He made me laugh every day. That was one of the reasons I loved him so much.

Now I stared at the clothes in my closet. *What should I wear?* I pulled out the red pantsuit with the matching three-quarter-length coat. Tony's favorite.

I smiled as I looked at my reflection in the mirror.

He certainly has good taste, I thought. Tony was very generous. Twice a year Tony and I visited New York City to shop for me. He loved presenting himself as a fashionista.

When Tony arrived home at 6:00 p.m., he noticed the lingering smell of his mother's "gravy" I'd been cooking. He walked into the dining room and his jaw dropped. "I am so sorry," he told me. "I had no idea that you were preparing such a romantic meal." He paused and sighed. "I already told our friends that we would meet them at the bar for drinks. "It will be a great meal this weekend. Let's invite Amy and David over for dinner. That will give you a chance to enjoy Mackenzie."

The thought of entertaining my daughter, son-in-law, and baby granddaughter filled me with excitement. "Of course," I said. "That's okay. We'll have a good time tonight."

Before going to the restaurant, we stopped at Moore Brothers Wine Company on DuPont Street in Wilmington, Delaware, not far from our home. Our friend John was part owner, so we dropped in for a quick hello.

A few years prior, John had hosted wine trips through Italy and France. Since Tony and I were avid wine enthusiasts, we went on both trips. The tours went from morning to midnight each day, in which we visited vineyards and participated in numerous wine tastings. Though we hadn't known any of the other ten couples in our group, by the end of each trip, we were the best of friends with most of them. Not only was the wine delicious, the food was the best of the best in Italian cooking. I gained ten pounds in ten days on our Italy vacation.

Now we stepped into the store and spotted John immediately, helping a customer. As soon as he could, he came over and greeted us. "Hey, I've got another tour coming up, through France," he told us. "October 2002."

"Count us in," Tony said. "We'll go. Let us know the dates."

I sighed happily at the thought. We had not planned a vacation for 2002, so France was the perfect escape.

The wine store was close enough to the restaurant that we opted just to walk. As we walked through the chilly night, we reminisced about our previous wine tours and were thrilled that we only had to wait ten months to enjoy France and our favorite city, Paris.

We did not have a reservation at the restaurant, and we arrived to find it seated to capacity. Tony put our names on the waiting list, and then we sat at the bar. He ordered his usual martini, in addition to ordering a bottle of wine.

We were finally seated and ordered. The evening lasted longer than expected. We knew many people at the restaurant, and we had numerous conversations throughout our meal. Tony ordered a second and third martini, as well as a second bottle of wine. Each bottle cost $120.

I didn't like how much he was spending—but I'd learned early in our marriage not to question Tony and his spending habits, or his excessive drinking. Although he was a heavy drinker, he rarely appeared drunk.

Nevertheless, we had a lovely evening together.

The following morning, Thursday, December 13, I awoke to find Tony getting ready to head out the door.

"You're up early," I said, still feeling the effects of the previous night's alcohol.

"Yeah, I want to get in to work," he said, the stress returning to his demeanor. "I've got a lot of work to do."

I noticed he was wearing khaki pants and a plaid shirt that he should have donated to Goodwill many years ago. It was very unusual for him to dress so poorly.

His closet was filled with expensive, hand-tailored suits, each costing between $4000 to $5,000. His shirts were $250 each, and he paid $1,000 for each pair of shoes. He paid cash for it all. He paid cash for everything. He always carried $1,000 or more. Of course, they were all $100 bills. Tony's signature was to leave a $100 tip for a $100 meal. Bartenders and servers lined up to wait on him. His family business paid for his Mercedes Benz, country club, and vacations around the world.

I once caught a glimpse at his W2, which claimed he earned $50,000 a year. Tony was always very private concerning his money and expenses, and insisted on having all of his bills mailed to his company. He said it was easier to take care of at work. I was clearly suspicious—but not enough to confront him over it.

I did confront him over his choice of dress this morning, however. "Why are you wearing those old clothes?"

"I'm working in the warehouse today," he said, brushing it off.

That sounds crazy. He rarely visits the warehouse, I thought. The family business included Tony and two other family members. They also employed ten people to work in the warehouse, sorting automotive parts. Tony had a reputation in his industry for being the one who never got his hands dirty.

I kissed him goodbye and told him to have a good day. "Oh, don't forget, we're meeting Joe tonight for dinner at Sullivan's. Would you like to meet at home so we can drive together, or do you want to meet at the restaurant?"

Tony nodded. "I'll meet you there."

I was looking forward to the evening. Joe and his wife, Gail, were good friends of ours. We'd met them at the Brandywine Country Club where we were members. Joe loved playing golf more than he loved working, so he had decided to take an early retirement and move to Hernando, Florida. He was in town to sign off on the paperwork for the sale of his company, while Gail stayed home to enjoy the Florida sun. So we invited him to join us for a meal before he left.

Promptly at 6:00 p.m., I arrived at Sullivan's Restaurant in Wilmington, about twenty minutes from our house. I looked around and spotted Joe but not Tony. Joe and I moved into the bar and ordered drinks while we waited for Tony to arrive. After one hour and no phone call, we started to worry.

I called Greg, the concierge at the building where we lived, to see if Tony was home.

"No," he said. "But a detective visited earlier today, looking for you. He asked about your husband."

Detective? I wondered why a detective would be looking for me.

"The detective asked me to tell you to come home and notify him once I spoke to you," Greg continued. "Your son-in-law and the detective want to meet with you as soon as possible."

A knot formed in my stomach. My son-in-law was a K9 county police officer.

"I have to go," I told Joe and filled him in on my conversation with the concierge. He immediately paid the bill, and we quickly exited the restaurant.

Joe walked me to my car. "Stay calm and drive carefully. I will be right behind you."

"Thank you, Joe." I felt comfort knowing that whatever was in front of me when I arrived home, I did not have to endure on my own. But what exactly *was* waiting for me?

Frantic, I tried calling my son-in-law, David, and my daughter, Amy. Both phones rang and rang.

"Pick up, pick up," I said into the phone, then hung up when they both went to voicemail.

I became angry. I felt so alone and needed the comfort of my family. *Where is Amy? Why is she not answering her phone?*

A million thoughts went through my mind as I drove. In my wildest imagination, I could not summon a reason for a detective to want to talk to me. Worst-case scenarios flooded my thoughts. *Did something happen to Tony? Or Amy? Or my granddaughter?*

My heart started to pound, and I found myself in the middle of a panic attack. To make matters worse, I felt an asthma attack coming on.

Keeping one hand tightly on the steering wheel, as I noticed the road was a bit icy, I felt blindly around in my purse on the passenger seat to locate my inhaler. As soon as I felt it, I pulled it out and used it immediately. At least that helped me breathe better. But it didn't alleviate the fear of the unknown.

When I arrived home, I parked my car in an underground assigned parking space and rushed to the front of the building to meet Joe, who had parked in the guest parking lot. I had rented office space for my jewelry business on the ground floor of the condominium building where we lived. I refused to go to my condo. Joe and I waited in my office, since it had a clear view of the parking lot. But as I waited, still not knowing anything, I felt as though I was going crazy.

It seemed as though it took hours for anybody to arrive. And as I waited, I continued to call David and Amy. But still, neither one answered their phone.

David finally arrived wearing his police uniform. A man dressed in a suit accompanied him.

I ran out to the lobby crying and screaming for answers. "David, what is going on? Where is Amy? Why is she not answering my calls?"

"Let's talk upstairs," he said as he took me by my arm and hurried me to the elevator with the detective.

As soon as we got into our condo, David asked me to sit on the sofa. The detective sat on my left side, and David sat on my right.

"Your husband is Anthony Grillo, correct?" the detective asked.

"Yes," I said, confused about why he would be asking me such a question when David was right there, and we all knew the answer.

"Your husband had an accident," the detective told me. "He is dead.".

I couldn't believe what I was hearing. "Dead? My husband is dead? No!" I shouted in disbelief. *He can't be dead . . .* Then I thought about the roads. They had been icy as I drove home. He must have been in a car accident on the way to meeting Joe and me.

The detective took my hand. "Your husband committed suicide. His body was found at the Delaware Veteran Memorial Cemetery in Sussex County around 1:00 p.m."

I immediately turned to David. "Is that true?"

David looked uncomfortable as he nodded. "Yes, it's true. Amy and Mackenzie are on their way. They'll be here shortly."

I screamed in disbelief as agony filled my heart and mind. "How did he die?"

The detective paused, as though he hated giving up that information to a grieving wife. "A gunshot wound to his head."

I shook my head again in disbelief. *That's impossible. Tony hated guns. He always said so.*

Tony's uncle John was a veteran. He had committed suicide just four years earlier, on October 27, 1997. Police discovered Tony's body in a gazebo not too far from his uncle's grave.

Even that news stunned me. Tony had never been a fan of his uncle John. By his family's standards, Uncle John was a loser. The family referred to him as a lowlife because he constantly asked Tony and his father for money.

Shortly afterward, Amy and my six-month-old granddaughter, Mackenzie, arrived with an overnight bag. A police officer had escorted them to my home.

"Mom!" Amy dropped the bag just inside the door and rushed to me. "What's going on? David called me and said that Tony was in an accident. He said, 'Your mother needs you now!' But he wouldn't tell me anything else."

David took her aside and gave her the news.

"Oh, Mom!" she threw her arms around me. I trembled in her arms and collapsed on the sofa. We cried in each other's arms for hours and spoke no words. We were too weak to talk.

I felt so grateful that she was there with me, refusing to leave my side.

Throughout the night and, into the next morning, family members on both sides arrived one by one. One of them sat in a chair by me and clapped his hands together. "That's it," he said, matter-of-factly. "It's over. He's gone. What's next?"

I withered into a state of shock. My sister, Billie, grew concerned and called a friend who was a doctor. Soon he arrived to administer a sedative and leave a prescription.

Why is he even here to torment me like this? I thought. He did not shed one tear the entire time. Tony had told me at one time not long before this that a family member at the business had been questioning him about the accounting books that Tony oversaw. He requested a meeting to discuss this concern.

Now this person sat so callously in our condo, I wondered if he had found significant discrepancies in the bookkeeping or even found a second book where Tony kept track of all the money he was "borrowing" from the company. Had he confronted him and told him that he was going to have him arrested?

Was that why Tony killed himself? I thought. Tony and his family were very proud people. His parents were full-blood Italians. His mother was born in Italy; his father in Sicily. Death must have seemed easier than shaming himself and especially shaming "The Family."

I fell into a fitful sleep on the sofa, exhausted from the nonstop crying and the double-dose of anxiety medication I took. I woke up at 4:00 a.m. to find my head resting on my daughter's lap. I was not aware of how long I slept.

My mind appeared to be in a fog. I was not aware of my surroundings.

"Mom, I'm here," Amy declared with tears streaming down her cheeks. "Mackenzie is here, too. David went home to feed the dog and to sleep. He'll be back tomorrow."

I looked around the room and saw my sisters and their families. Some of them arrived after I fell asleep and refused to leave until they had an opportunity to console me. They wanted to make sure I knew they were there. Joe left shortly after my family arrived.

After everyone eventually left, Amy and I sat on the sofa and talked for hours in the dark while Mackenzie slept quietly in my bed. I simply couldn't wrap my head around my husband's death. Why? I wondered over and over.

"Mom, I'm not sure what to say to you. I can't find the words. None of this makes sense to me."

I appreciated my daughter's honesty and willingness to comfort me.

"Let's get some sleep," she said. "Tomorrow is going to be a hectic day."

I woke up three hours later when I heard Mackenzie crying. I did not open my bedroom door. I sat up in bed and let my own tears come. My body felt limp, and I could barely move. I just wanted to be by myself.

A thousand thoughts rushed through my mind. *My husband is dead, and I do not have a clue why. He shot himself in his head? He hates guns. His death makes absolutely no sense. I thought our marriage was great. He called me twice a day and told me that he loved me. If he was depressed, I didn't see it. Oh God, why didn't you show me signs that he was depressed? If you had, I could have helped Tony.*

And then my distress turned to anger, as I turned my rage on Him. *It's your fault, God, that he is dead.*

Now I truly felt lost and alone. Empty. *Where do I go from here?*

How could I make anybody understand that I felt as though someone had ripped my heart out of my body. For a split second, I thought taking my own life would be the only way to rid myself of this unbearable pain.

But my rational mind took over. *No, I could never put my daughter and family through the kind of pain that I am going through now.*

Fortunately, and unfortunately, the only one who *could* help me get through my pain and suffering and help me become whole again was the one whom I hated most right then . . . God.

If you're brave enough to say goodbye, life will reward you with a new hello.
—Paulo Coelho

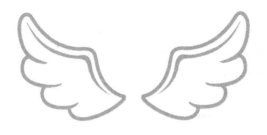

CHAPTER 2

THE FIRST DAY OF THE REST OF MY LIFE

It hurts when you have someone in your heart, but you can't hold them in your arms.
—Anonymous

At 7:00 a.m. I heard a soft knock on my bedroom door. "Mom, are you awake?" Amy said as she quietly peeked around the door.

I was sitting up in bed, feeling the weight of exhaustion from the night before. I started to cry. "Did I have a horrible dream or did Tony die by suicide? Did he really shoot himself in his head?"

Her face filled with concern. "Yes, Mom. I am so sorry." She stood awkwardly in the doorway, and I could tell that she wanted to help me but wasn't sure how. "Why don't you just stay in bed for a little while and relax. I'll get you some coffee. Would you like me to get Mackenzie and put her in bed with you?"

"That would be very nice," I replied. Having my sweet six-month-old granddaughter close to me might help take away some of the anguish I was feeling.

Amy disappeared and within a few moments brought a sleeping Mackenzie into the room and gently placed her on the bed, then she left again to get our coffee.

Carrying two steaming hot cups of coffee, Amy joined us on the bed where she and I talked for hours as Mackenzie slept peacefully between us.

Soon the phone began to ring. I knew it was people who wanted to hear the news or to offer their condolences, but I just wasn't up for talking with anybody quite yet. Amy quickly answered and told the person on the other line, "My mother is sleeping right now. I know you want to see her. It would be best if you come anytime in the afternoon. Also, can you please call everyone in your family and tell them the same?"

At around 9:00 a.m., David arrived. He joined us in the bedroom and sat in a chaise lounge in the corner. "How are you feeling?" he asked.

"I'm sick to my stomach and would like to stay in bed all day."

"That would be nice, Mom," Amy said, "but your family has been calling all morning to make sure that you are okay, and they want to stop by and see you."

I dreaded it, though I knew she was right.

"David, give me a better understanding of how and when you found out about Tony," Amy asked.

Excusing myself, I went to the bathroom, feeling unsure that I was up for hearing any more details right then. I looked in the mirror and saw a sallow disheveled woman looking back at me. *I look disgusting. I need to pull myself together before I meet with anyone.*

I didn't know why I was so concerned about my appearance, especially after what I had gone through the last eighteen hours. Maybe because I needed something to distract me.

"I'm going to take a shower and put some makeup on so I can feel a little better about myself," I said as I peeked my head out of the bathroom door. "Please fix me another cup of coffee."

"Okay," Amy said. "David and I will be in the kitchen, if you need us." They left Mackenzie sleeping on my bed.

Before I could get into the shower, I heard a knock on my front door. I was surprised since the building's policy requires the concierge to call first to announce that a guest is in the building to visit, but I did not receive a call.

I was tempted to ignore it and just get into the shower, but curiosity got the best of me. I trudged slowly to the front door and opened it. There stood my good friends Meg and Craig, who lived in the same building.

"Meg! Craig! What are you doing here? I thought you were at your other home." They owned a house in Chatham, Massachusetts, and had been staying there. I stood out of the way so they could enter.

"We were," Meg said, as they both stepped into the condo. "The concierge called us and told us about Tony's death."

"We immediately booked a flight for this morning."

"But why are you here?"

"Where else would we be?" Meg said. "You're our friend. We need to be with you."

I was amazed by their act of kindness. They have important jobs as a partner of a finance company and executive vice president of a major insurance corporation. They walked away from their busy schedules to support me in my time of trauma.

"We're going upstairs," Meg said, "but we will stop by later." Then she hugged me tightly and we cried in each other's arms.

After they left, I returned to the bathroom and took a shower and got ready for the day.

At 10:00 a.m. I received a call from Greg, the concierge. "Tony's parents, Mr. and Mrs. Grillo are here to see you."

My heart sank into my stomach. They had already lost one child from SIDS (Sudden Infant Death Syndrome)—their first daughter, Virginia, in 1941, when she was only one year old. I knew the grief I was feeling, but I couldn't imagine being a parent and having to bury not one but two children—especially one to suicide. "Please escort them to the elevator."

I stepped outside of the condo and met them at the elevator. As soon as the elevator doors opened, I saw the sad look on their faces. Their eyes were bloodshot from crying.

We silently walked to my condo where Amy and David greeted us at the door.

They refused to sit.

"My son is dead. Do you know of any reason why he killed himself?" my mother-in-law asked.

"I am just as confused as you are," I told her.

"Was he depressed? Had you been fighting? Did he say anything to you to give you a warning that he needed help?"

Her questions came at me so quickly, I stopped trying to answer them. Nothing I could say would bring her comfort—or bring back our Tony.

Her face grew flushed and she wobbled as she started to collapse. David quickly ushered her to the nearest chair. My father-in-law sat in the chair next to her. He did not ask any questions.

After only about ten minutes, he stood. "Anna, let's go. I cannot stand to be here anymore." They both exited without another word.

"What just happened?" I asked Amy and David after my in-laws left. "My mother-in-law's questions made me feel like they're blaming me for Tony's death. I am just as confused as they are." Then I silently wondered, *Why did my father-in-law say, "I cannot stand to be here anymore?" None of this makes sense.*

A half-hour later, three more family members arrived.

"Hello, Janet," Jason said and gave me a kiss on the cheek. He immediately sat in the same chair where he'd sat only a few hours before. Zachary and his wife, Sarah, leaned in to me for a group hug. The strange thing was that I was the only one crying.

"I gotta be honest, we're angry with Anthony and cannot imagine why he killed himself. We want you to know that we are here for you; all you have to do is ask. Jason and I have a lot to do at work, but Sarah will stay with you and help you with the funeral arrangements and the cemetery plot."

Wow, that's nice. I thought back to something Tony had told me six months before. He'd mentioned that if anything ever happened to him, I should contact his family, and they would be there for me. His comment had struck me as odd at the time, and I asked him why he'd said that. "We never know when we will die," he'd only said.

"Sarah, I am very grateful that you stopped by and are willing to help me with the funeral and burial arrangements," I said.

"Of course," she told me.

Jason and Zachary didn't stay long, and when they left for work, true to her word, Sarah remained behind. Another family member, Christine, arrived shortly afterward.

"Hello, Janet, how are you feeling?"

"I'm doing a little better than yesterday. I took a double dose of anxiety medication."

"I know we could all use some of those drugs," she said.

Christine was there to help as well. So they went right to work, making phone calls and getting the arrangements started, leaving nothing else for me to do except rest. No one else from Tony's large family visited or called.

That's strange, I thought and could not imagine why they would not stop by to see me or, at the very least, give me a call. Though we weren't particularly close, and I always had the distinct impression that they didn't like me, I had been a member of the Grillo family for more than thirteen years. And I *was* Tony's widow.

With nothing left to do, I called the concierge to thank him for being there for me the day before and for everything that he had done, and to alert him that many people would be visiting today, and that he could simply let them come up without phoning each time.

"Absolutely, Mrs. Grillo," Greg replied. "We are here for you. Whatever you need, just ask. By the way, your sister Bobbie and her husband, Tommy, just arrived. I'll escort them to the elevator."

Bobbie came in and gave me a big hug. "I'm so sorry," she said. "How can I help?"

I shrugged. "There's nothing much for you to do. Sarah and Christine are handling it all."

Bobbie raised her eyebrows. Bobbie is a take-charge person. She is tiny and mighty and had a reputation of being a force not to be reckoned with. She left me in the living room with Tommy while she walked into the kitchen where the women were.

After a few moments I heard her voice boom out. "What are you talking about?"

"Nothing." Sarah's voice sounded startled, as though she'd been caught doing something wrong.

Bobbie's voice turned angry. "Did I just hear you talking about Tony having an affair?"

Neither said another word. I stepped into the kitchen to see what the commotion was all about.

Bobbie grabbed the paperwork out of Sarah's hand, defiantly making a bold statement. "That's it; you've completed your task. I suggest that you both leave and never come back. Something is wrong, and Janet does not need to be made aware of it at this time."

"We're here to help with the funeral arrangements," Sarah said.

"I guess you did not hear me the first time. I want you to leave and never come back. I am in charge now!"

After they left, I looked at Bobbie. "What did they say about Tony and what . . . ?"

"Nothing. Just gossip. You don't need to worry about it."

My mind was too garbled to think clearly. *I can't worry about what-*

ever that was right now.

"I'm going to write Tony's obituary, okay?" Bobbie said. After a little while she brought me a sheet of paper with writing on it. "Here, give this a read," she told me. "What do you think?"

I focused my eyes on the writing. "Anthony J. Grillo, age fifty-seven of Park Plaza, died on Thursday, December 13, 2001. Mr. Grillo was president of Quality Automotive Parts. He was a 1963 graduate of Salesianum High School and attended Goldey Beacon College. He was a sports fan and enjoyed playing golf. He is survived by his wife, Janet V. Grillo . . ."

My heart shattered. I couldn't believe I was sitting here and reading my husband's obituary. I looked back over it. "Enjoyed playing golf," I read and shut my eyes. We were members at the Brandywine Country Club in Wilmington and had become good friends with many golfing members, especially on the nineteenth hole. Joe and Gail were two of our closest friends. I used to play golf with Tony, but he stopped playing with me one on one when I consistently beat his score.

I opened my eyes and looked at Bobbie. "This is great. Thank you."

Throughout the day, many friends stopped by to pay their respects. Two very close friends, Jay and Denise, walked into my home and immediately started to cry.

"This is unbelievable," Jay said. "I talked with Tony yesterday. We made plans to have dinner this weekend. His death makes absolutely no sense."

I nodded, remembering how Tony had promised we'd eat my homemade Italian dinner together that weekend too.

"Let's go into your bedroom and talk," Jay said, leaning in. "There are too many people out here."

The three of us walked into my bedroom, and Denise closed the doors behind us.

"You look like hell. Let's relax and lay on the bed and talk." The three of us lay down and then cried some more. We spoke very little, but

I was grateful that they were there with me. Their presence assured me that everything would be okay.

Finally, Jay broke the silence. "Janet, do you need any money? I will give you anything that you want." Jay was very successful and had several homes, a sixty-foot yacht, a talking parrot named Bert, and expensive cars. He was also one of the most generous people I knew.

Without hesitation, I asked, "Will you give me your Maserati?"

We all started laughing.

"Oh no," he said. "Not my Maserati."

I did not want Jay's expensive car. I was searching for something corny to bring laughter into the stressed atmosphere. Jay and Denise had invited me and Tony and Joe and Gail to their home in Florida for New Year's. *Now all those plans . . .*

"We would still like to have you visit with us," Denise said. "And we will not take no for an answer."

"That would be nice," I told them. "It will give me something to look forward to." But the truth was that my heart was not in it.

Everyone left my home by 6:00 p.m., except for Amy, David, and Mackenzie. We drank wine and enjoyed the food that many people brought with them when they visited.

Even though I was drinking wine, David insisted that I continue taking my anxiety medication. He witnessed the change in my demeanor when the drugs started to wear off. I noticed a change in my demeanor, too. I found that as the drugs were leaving my body, I experienced uncomfortable physical, mental, and emotional withdraw combined with uncontrollable shaking.

Witnessing a broken woman was hard on everyone. From that point on, David insisted on doubling my medication.

At 8:00 p.m., Amy announced that it was time for me to go to bed. "Let's go, Mom. I will help you get ready." She helped me undress and get into my nightgown. Parenting a parent is not one of any child's responsibility that they would look forward to doing, especially for a parent who was only fifty-two years old. My heart ached that I had put her in this position, though I knew she wouldn't have it any other way. *She's such a good girl.* Her kindness gave me much comfort.

"How about I lie next to you for a while? Just till you fall asleep?" Amy knew that I was afraid to be by myself.

"I'd like that. Thank you."

"We have a busy day tomorrow. We have an appointment at McCrery Funeral Home to choose a casket and discuss the funeral arrangements."

As Amy rattled off our to-do list, I silently asked God, *How am I going to make it through the next few days?* I should have asked, *How am I going to make it through the rest of my life?* but I wasn't ready to face that huge of a question.

But other questions kept pushing to the forefront of my mind. *There is something unusual going on with Tony's family.* I could not put my finger on it. *Why were Sarah and Christine whispering in the kitchen? What did Bobbie overhear that she refused to discuss with me? Why did I not receive any phone calls from the rest of the people in Tony's family?* I could not imagine Tony's family not being there for me, especially when I needed them the most.

After Amy left the bedroom, my mind continued to wander through the events of the past two days and tears came again. "Please, God, give me strength to get through the next few days." Again, I wasn't sure why I asked for strength for only a few days; I should have asked for more. I should have asked for strength for a lifetime of tomorrows.

Amy knocked on my door at 8:00 a.m. "Time to get up, sleepy-head. Our appointment at McCrery's is at 11:00 a.m. I'll fix your coffee. Would you like an English muffin too?"

"That would be great," I said.

Getting dressed to go to the funeral home was like getting dressed for my own funeral. When we arrived, the owner, Jay McCrery, greeted us. He and his wife, Pam, were clients when I worked at Stuart Kingston Jewelers in Wilmington many years before.

"I am sorry for your loss," he told me. "Please follow me to my office. We can talk in private."

As we sat in his office, I could smell the essence of flowers and death at the same time. Thank God that tissues were available on every table. Much crying was on my list. Jay explained the process of the viewing and funeral. "Your husband is here. Would you like to see him?"

"Absolutely not. I will wait for the viewing." Honestly, I was afraid to see him. When Amy and I visited the funeral home, we took the clothes that he would be buried in. For some reason, though I knew I was wrong in my thinking, I envisioned him wearing bloody clothes and could not bear the thought of seeing a hole in his head.

"Would you like the casket to be opened or closed?"

What in the world is he asking? How can he ask if I want the casket open, knowing that my husband shot himself in the head?

"I think it would be best if the casket is closed. You can keep it open for the family to view only. It would be best for friends not to view, though." I paused, unsure how to broach the subject of Tony's head wound. "I am curious," I finally continued. "How would you display his body with a hole in his head?"

Jay frowned slightly and apologetically. "Unfortunately, this is not the first time we have had a service for someone who has died by suicide, in the same manner, that your husband died. Instead of laying his body to the normal position of left, we will lay his head at the right side of the casket."

"Thank you," I said simply.

Amy helped me select a top-of-the-line casket. I think I chose it for the name. The "Regal" was a stainless-steel casket that had a sophisticated look and color, which added a touch of elegance. I thought the natural platinum finish and pearl velvet interior would be perfect. It was the ideal choice to lay Tony for his final resting place.

When Amy and I left the funeral home, we sat in the car for a few minutes to collect ourselves and to review the casket choice and funeral arrangements. We wanted to be certain we did not overlook anything. Just as we were getting ready to leave, I noticed one of Tony's family members exiting the funeral home.

I lowered my car window. "Why are you here?"

"I wanted to see Anthony and check on the funeral arrangements," he told me, looking surprised that I'd seen him.

That's very strange. Why does he feel the need to see Anthony?

I noticed he was carrying a small black book, but I couldn't tell exactly what it was.

After he got into his car, I could have kicked myself that I failed to ask him about it. *Why do I get the feeling that Tony's family is hiding something?*

On December 18, 2001, Amy, David, and I arrived at the funeral home at 5:00 p.m. I wanted to be the first there to have a private moment with my husband. I discreetly entered a room filled with more than fifty flower arrangements. I was afraid to walk directly up to the casket and decided to take a tour of the place, reading the cards attached to each flower arrangement.

Monsignor Lemon was in the room. He was the head priest at Immaculate Heart of Mary Church. Tony and I attended mass two to three times a month. Though I'd met Monsignor Lemon on a few occasions, I did not know him personally. When I got closer to him, I thanked him for being there.

He quickly grabbed my hand and shook it with jubilation. "It's so lovely to see you. How have you been?"

This man is crazy. He must not know who I am and only recognizes me by sight. "Well, Monsignor Lemon, considering that is my husband lying in the casket, I guess you can say that I am not doing very well!"

His face immediately went bright red. "I am so sorry for your loss, and very sorry that I did not recognize you. May God be with you and your family."

I thanked him and turned toward the casket. I'd procrastinated enough, now it was time to see my husband.

Tony had his head lying on the right side of the casket, just as Jay had promised, so that the wound was on the other side and covered up. Although my curiosity got the best of me, I did not look at that side to see if I could spot the wound. I was already traumatized and did not want to cause myself additional pain.

He looks so handsome and at peace. I always liked that suit and tie. Seeing Tony in the suit reminded me of our shopping trips to Boyd's, one of the country's top independent luxury fashion stores, in Philadelphia. Tony was a regular customer. All the salesmen knew him by name and lined up to assist him with his purchases. For each $5,000 suit he purchased, he also purchased two shirts and two ties. Because his dress appearance always had to be perfect, the salesman color coded each outfit.

Emotions washed over me then. *God, how can I love and hate this man at the same time? Why, Tony? Why did you kill yourself?*

I knelt before Tony for more than ten minutes. I knew this would be the last time I would ever see him again. When I went to stand, my legs felt weak. David was immediately at my side, helping me stand.

"Let's go into a private room where you can sit without anyone bothering you," he said. "I will get you some water, and I think it would be best if you took another pill. You need to be more relaxed."

"Thank you, David. Please keep an eye on me tonight and help me if you see me wavering."

I sat in the room for more than a half hour before going to the ladies' room to freshen up. Taking a double dose of anxiety medication did not allow me to think clearly. When I realized we needed to close the casket with family members present, I started to panic. I knew that the coffin could not be closed until I was attending.

When I walked out of the ladies' room, I noticed a long line of people waiting to pay their respects. I quickly went back into the viewing room to discover that the casket was still open, and the viewing had already begun.

What is going on? I told the funeral director that I wanted a closed casket.

I immediately went to the funeral director's assistant and demanded that the casket be closed. "I specifically requested that my husband's casket be closed."

"I spoke with Jay. After you left the funeral home, one of Tony's family members visited and demanded that the casket be open." It appeared that the one I saw outside the funeral home a few days before had lied to me about why he visited the funeral home.

I could not believe my eyes. I was embarrassed for Tony that others would view him in the open casket. He was a very vain person and would not want people to see him that way.

I stood in line with the rest of the family and kept my mouth shut, just as the wife of an Italian should do. The temperature was forty-seven degrees, and it was pouring down rain. It was a perfect setting for a viewing. More than one thousand people lined up in the rain to pay their respects. Many were shocked when they saw an open casket. I viewed people walking away shaking their heads and overheard comments, "If that were my husband, his casket would definitely be closed. Tony would be mortified if he knew he was being viewed."

The funeral home scheduled the viewing from 7:00 to 9:00 p.m. Because of the number of people, the viewing did not end until 11:00 p.m. I knew many people there, though many were strangers to me. I'd been Tony's wife for more than a decade. How could I not know so many? *Who are all of these people? How did they know Tony? Who are the group of men gathered together wearing long trench coats, dripping in gold and diamonds, and even wearing sunglasses inside?*

I took my place in the receiving line with Tony's two daughters and family standing to my left. We did not talk because we were overwhelmed with the endless line of people consoling us.

I was surprised when Tony's ex-wife, approached me with tears in her eyes. She even hugged me, which strangely brought me comfort.

I focused my attention back on the guests I knew. One of them was Karen, with whom I played golf at Brandywine Country Club for many years. Her marriage ended in a divorce because her husband was very controlling. I remember that he not only selected the clothes she wore, he insisted that the top button was securely fastened on her golf shirts. Karen had walked away from our friendship, many years before, because she was dealing with too many issues on her own.

Now she stood in front of me. "Do you know who I am?"

"Yes, I do. My question is, how did you find out about Tony? And why are you here?"

I knew she now lived in New Jersey. She would not have found out by reading the obituary in a newspaper.

"I'm sorry that I have not kept in contact with you. Once you get settled after the funeral, give me a call. I have a lot to tell you about your husband and how his family will deal with you now. Know that I will stand by you and help in any way I can."

That's odd. Tony's death, family, viewing, funeral, and now a person I have not seen in three years has information that she wants to share about Tony?

It was becoming too much for me to handle, and once again I motioned to David that I needed to take another anxiety pill. That was the third one that I took in two hours. By the end of the evening, I was not feeling any pain. I was not feeling *anything*. We all went home to get some rest and prepare ourselves for the next day, the funeral.

The church scheduled the service for 11:00 a.m. The limousine arrived at my home at 10:30. Tony's daughters did not come until 10:45.

"Sorry we're late," they told me. "We thought the limousine was going to pick us up at our house."

"No worries, you're here now. One thing for sure is that the church service cannot begin until we arrive."

Amy, David, Tony's daughters, and their husbands rode in the limousine with me. We discussed the viewing and agreed that many people attended whom we did not know. We discussed the events planned for the day and all agreed that we would be glad when the day was over.

When we arrived at the church, we noticed that the parking lot was completely filled, and many cars were parked on the street and even some on the grass.

This is crazy, I thought. *I cannot believe that we were the last to arrive.*

Tony's daughters quickly joined their families, and David and Amy escorted me down the aisle. I was praying that I would start to reduce my anxiety medication; however, today was not that day. Although I looked like a bride escorted down the church aisle for all to view, I was not aware of the situation. Sisters later commented that I looked ridiculous. They did not realize that we were late in leaving, and that I needed support walking.

As soon as I sat down in the pew with David and Amy, my ex-husband walked across the aisle to console me, which I thought was a nice gesture. Tony's ex-wife sat in a nearby pew with her husband, daughters, and their families. We spoke no words. We acknowledged each other's presence—nothing more and nothing less.

The atmosphere in the church was very solemn. I held my composure through the service, but fell apart when they played "On Eagle's Wings" on the organ. I have always had trouble hearing that song, mostly since they played it at my mother's funeral service.

Only family and close friends attended the burial service. Tony's parents were the only people crying. Honestly, I had no tears left inside of me to shed. I was glad that Tony was at rest. *Now I must start working on Janet*, I thought.

Afterward, we all gathered at one of Tony's family member's house. It was a very dark setting. My mother-in-law and father-in-law sat in chairs in the living room and chose not to mingle or talk with anyone. I sat with my family and did not attempt to speak with anyone in Tony's family, nor did they attempt to speak with me.

I returned home to a quiet house. My daughter and granddaughter spent the night. I knew they, along with other members of my family, were afraid to leave me alone, so they took turns staying with me. After two nights of being surrounded by family, I insisted that I would be okay and asked everyone to leave.

When they all left, including Amy and David, I stood in the living room for a few moments and wondered what my life was going to look like from now on. I was all alone. I started to wean myself off the anxiety medication and stayed in bed most days. My body was exhausted, and my emotional state of mind was shallow.

With the holidays quickly approaching, I wasn't sure how I was going to manage. The next time that I would be with Tony's family would be on Christmas Eve. It was a Grillo tradition that his parents started many years before. It did not matter where anybody lived. On Christmas Eve, every member of the Grillo clan needed to celebrate with the family. My mother-in-law would accept nothing less.

For the next six days, I remained alone with only my memories to keep me company. As I thought back over the funeral, my curiosity piqued over Karen's presence and announcement that she needed to talk to me about Tony. Karen had married into an Italian family. After her divorce, her husband's family walked away from her, so I was sure she felt certain that Tony's family would do the same. But still, I wondered why she couldn't have just told me that? Was there something else?

What can she possibly know about my husband and his family that is such a secret?

I thought yesterday was the first day of the rest of my life but it turns out today is.

—Steve Martin

CHAPTER 3

CHRISTMAS EVE AND THE START OF A NEW YEAR

Do not wait until the conditions are perfect to begin.
Beginning makes the conditions perfect.
—Alan Cohen

I woke up Christmas Eve morning feeling sick. I wanted to stay in bed and erase the entire day before it started. I knew that was not an option. My family's tradition had always been to celebrate Christmas Eve and Christmas morning with our immediate family and gather together at one house for Christmas day dinner.

Knowing that I had the entire day in front of me, I saw no hurry to get out of bed. I enjoyed several cups of coffee and watched one of my favorite movies, *It's a Wonderful Life,* starring Jimmy Stewart and Donna Reed.

I watched as George Bailey, Jimmy Stewart's character, had so many problems that he thought about ending his life. As the angels discussed George, the movie presented flashbacks of his life. George decided that he was going to commit suicide by jumping off a bridge. At the moment he was ready to jump, he heard a man cry for help. He ended up rescuing his guardian angel, Clarence, who then showed George what his town would have looked like if it hadn't been for all the good deeds he'd done for others over the years.

I couldn't help but think about Tony. Then I smiled as the movie ended. It gave me a flutter of hope that we have angels watching over us and everything that happens to us is part of God's plan. That gave me the strength and courage to get out of bed to face the day's events.

I heard a knock on my door and was surprised to find my sisters Billie and Peggy holding a Christmas tree and decorations.

"What in the world are you doing here? You bought me a Christmas tree?"

"You got that right," Peggy said. "There is no way that you are going to miss Christmas."

I felt such amazing outpouring love from my sisters. I even felt that my deceased mother was standing right by their side when I heard Peggy speak my mother's favorite saying—"You got that right!" God gave me the gift of three angels—my sisters Billie and Peggy and my favorite guardian angel, Mom.

I cried as I welcomed them into my home. "This is wonderful," I told them from the bottom of my heart.

"Move out of our way," Peggy demanded. "Go and get ready for the day. By the time you take the two hours to fix your hair and put on your makeup, your house is going to look like Christmas."

For the first time in days, I laughed. *She is right about the time it takes me to get ready. I always enjoy the time I give myself.*

"And do not open your bedroom door until I come and get you, understand?" Billie told me.

After a while, Billie quietly knocked on my bedroom door. "Okay, it's time to start enjoying Christmas. Close your eyes, and I'll hold your hand to guide you."

As she led me slowly, I could hear Christmas music playing and then I caught the smell of a cinnamon candle and the Christmas tree.

"You are going to be so happy when you see what we have done," Billie said. "Open your eyes."

My sisters had darkened the living room so that the only lights shining were the red and green tear-shaped bulbs wrapped around the Christmas tree. Beautiful decorations were lovingly placed everywhere. My eyes immediately filled with tears.

"You are the best," I told them. "The tree and decorations are the most beautiful I have ever seen. Oh, my goodness, look at the red bow's size at the top in place of an angel. It's perfect. Thank you!"

Just below the bow sat two six-inch, crisp-starched, white cotton angels. "Oh!" My eyes filled with tears. I'd purchased those angels to represent our parents who both died on the same day—June 21—eleven years apart. Mom had been dead only two years. How I missed her. When she first died, I'd thought, *Heaven has gained another angel.* So I found those angels and purchased two each to represent our parents and presented them to each member of our family.

Now when I saw those angels, I felt comforted. "I'm so glad you added my mommy and daddy angels at the top of the tree."

Billie and Peggy left soon after to complete the things they needed to prepare for their Christmas Eve with their immediate families.

"Thanks again," I said as they were leaving. "I am very grateful and love you for doing this for me! I will see you tomorrow night for dinner."

Once they left, I realized that I needed to wrap Christmas gifts. Fortunately, I completed my shopping before Tony had died. I was hesitant to attend Christmas Eve dinner with Tony's family, because no one in the family appeared to be talking to me, except for my mother-in-law when I called her.

I thought again about the way they were avoiding me. *Well, maybe that's just how they are managing their own grief. Everybody needs to deal with their grief on their terms.*

Christmas Eve dinner was supposed to have been at my mother-in-law's home, but because she spent most of her time in her room since Anthony's death, Tony's cousin Ginger decided it would be best to have it at her house.

Ginger asked me to arrive at 4:00 p.m.

Christmas Eve was always my mother-in-law's favorite day of the year. Besides creating a feast of food for her family to enjoy, she also enjoyed showering everyone with expensive gifts.

Every year, Ginger and husband invited the family to their house for Christmas day brunch. When Tony (called Anthony in his family's presence) and I were first together, we were not invited to Christmas Eve dinners or Christmas day brunch.

After being together for three years, Ginger finally invited us to brunch—with conditions. Her invitation also included inviting Tony's ex-wife and her husband. The brunch started at 10:00 a.m. Ginger asked us to arrive at 1:00 p.m. We attended only once and decided we would create our own tradition of preparing brunch for my daughter and family and Tony's two daughters and family. We continued that tradition until Tony died.

I breathed in deeply now as I stood at Ginger's front door, carrying two large shopping bags filled with gifts for my mother-in-law, father-in-law, Tony's daughters, and their immediate families.

"Thank you for coming," Ginger said, as she welcomed me into her home. "We are so glad you are here."

"Me too," I said and tried to mean it. "I have been looking forward to this evening all week."

I was one of the last to arrive. *This is crazy. Ginger asked me to come at 4:00 p.m. By the look of things, everyone else arrived much earlier.* I looked around and saw the twelve-inch stainless steel bowl was only half full of the jumbo shrimp. The rest of the appetizers were half eaten already, and I spotted several empty bottles of champagne in the trashcan.

Ginger's brother, Jason, brought me a glass of champagne and invited me to sit next to him. "How are you doing?"

"Just about as good as the rest of the family," I admitted. "It is a very sad Christmas for all of us, especially for your parents. No parent should have to bury one child, let alone two."

Jason nodded. "Yes. They haven't spoken to anyone in a week."

"Where are they?" I hadn't seen them since I'd arrived.

He told me that they were sitting in the dark in the family room, then he excused himself to join his family.

I appreciated that he had taken time to talk to me and noticed that everyone else kept their distance.

Two people I noticed keeping their distance from me were Christine and Sarah. The last time I was this close to them was when Bobbie asked them to leave my house and never come back.

Though I was hesitant to speak with my in-laws, feeling afraid because of how they'd acted the last time they'd come to my condo, I knew I needed to greet them. *They asked me many questions, and I did not have any answers.*

I timidly walked into the room and saw them seated next to each other. "Hello, Mom and Dad, how are you feeling?"

My mother-in-law did not say a word.

"How do you think we are?" my father-in-law said, an edge to his voice. "Our son is dead, and we do not have a clue why he killed himself."

"Unfortunately, we all have many questions and no answers."

When they gave no response, I took it as my cue to excused myself. "Our friends Jay and Denise invited Anthony and me to Florida to play golf and celebrate the New Year. They insisted that I keep my plans in place. I will be leaving on December 28 and will return on January 5. I'll stop by to see you when I get home."

My mother-in-law wiped tears from her eyes. "Okay."

My father-in-law simply waved his hand to acknowledge.

I'd had my fill of how much I could take. Had they forgotten that I was the grieving widow? That my pain was just as deep—if not more so? As I re-entered the main room, I felt distinctly that I was no longer welcome. It was time to leave, even without having dinner or saying goodbye. As I approached the front door to exit, I noticed Tony's two daughters with their families in the living room.

In unison, both daughters saw me and asked, "Where are you going? Aren't you going to stay for dinner?"

"My stomach is upset. I think I should go home. By the way, I left your presents under the tree. You will especially like one gift. Your father created it especially for you."

Tony loved his children and grandchildren dearly. The gifts he had selected were fourteen-karat yellow gold lockets with a decorative chain. Enclosed in the lockets were photos of their children. I did not wait around for them to open anything.

I was in bed by 8:00 p.m. As rough as the evening part had been, I still felt immense gratitude. "Thank you, God, for getting me through today," I declared out loud. "Please stand with me as I face every tomorrow." I was not sure if God was listening, but I prayed that He was.

Amy and David invited me to spend the night, but I declined. I anticipated the Christmas Eve dinner celebration lasting much longer than it did, and I did not have the heart to call Amy and tell her what had transpired. She would have insisted that I spend the night with her.

At 8:30 a.m. Christmas morning, my phone rang. "Merry Christmas, Mom," Amy said, sounding happy. "I was calling to see how your evening went, and to invite you to our house for breakfast. I know it's last minute, but I hope you'll come."

"That would be great," I said and meant it. I needed something to take my mind off the previous evening. "We can talk about last night when I see you. I'll be over around 9:30, is that okay?"

"Perfect. We'll have a Bloody Mary ready for you when you arrive."

"Just what my doctor would have ordered. See you soon."

I arrived to find Amy and David still in their pajamas. Part of their Christmas tradition was to wear matching PJs. Even Mackenzie was wearing a one-piece from the same designer—J C Penney. "Oolala. Way too cute. Is this design from France?" I said, laughing.

"Mais oui. Direct from J C Penne," Amy said, giving a twirl.

We enjoyed a couple of Bloody Marys as we sat next to a roaring fire. The warmth felt good as the outside temperature was 35 degrees—chilly enough for a fire, but not cold enough for the snow of a white Christmas.

As our laughter died down, we all settled into an uneasiness. I think we all realized we needed to talk about the elephant in the room.

"How are you feeling, and how did it go last night?" David asked. Even though he was my son-in-law, he had a bit of that police officer interrogation bit going on. I didn't mind, though, since I was proud of him and his career. In addition to being a K-9 police officer, he had been a K-9 handler in the Air Force, and even had the opportunity to work on Air Force One.

"I feel a little better each day. Obviously, this Christmas season has been stressful. I thought I imagined the distance of Tony's family, but I discovered it was not my imagination." I went on to detail the previous evening's events with my in-laws.

"Mom, I am so sorry they treated you so poorly," Amy said. "I hope you didn't stay."

"I didn't. I decided not to stay for dinner after I spoke to Tony's parents."

"Let's do this," Amy suggested after I told them everything. "Let's agree not to talk about Tony or his family for the rest of the day."

"I think that's an excellent decision," I said.

We opened our Christmas gifts while enjoying the smell of coffee, cinnamon buns, and eggs benedict. I left their house around 1:00 p.m. to go home and relax before going to my family's Christmas dinner at Bobbie and Tommy's house.

I was one of the first guests to arrive. Tommy greeted me at the door with a warm hello and hug. It felt so different from the previous night. "So glad you are a little early," he said. "I was looking for an excuse to start drinking, but I didn't want to start on my own."

I laughed. "Not having a drinking companion never stopped you before. Anyway, I have you beat. I've been drinking since 10:00 a.m."

As I entered the kitchen, I noticed an open bottle of red wine and three balloon-stem wine glasses correctly filled for the wine to breathe. Tommy was kidding about waiting to drink. He poured a glass for me before I arrived.

"You look very nice," Bobbie said. "How are you feeling?"

"Much better now that I am with my own family. I'm looking forward to a fun-filled evening."

Two by two, family members arrived. Before long, all seventeen members squeezed into the kitchen-family room area and enjoyed drinks and appetizers. I was grateful that no one talked about Tony, my in-laws, or my Christmas Eve dinner. When Amy, David, and Mackenzie came, everyone's attention focused on Mackenzie. She was the first baby born in our family, so everyone couldn't wait for their turn to hold her.

"How are you holding up?" Amy asked.

"Good. I'm really glad no one has asked me anything about Tony or his family."

She smiled wistfully. "I called everybody and asked them not to."

"Thank you."

Throughout an amazing and delicious dinner and for the rest of the evening, I felt as though I was having a very normal Christmas celebration. But deep down, I knew I wasn't. Even not wanting to discuss Tony didn't remove him from my thoughts. I still ached over his absence and over what he'd done.

After dinner, Bobbie declared, "Now let the fun begin." It was time for our favorite part of the evening, what we called the Chinese auction, similar to what some families call a white elephant gift exchange. Each person brought a gift and then we all picked a piece of paper that contained a number to identify the order of selecting those gifts. When a person's turn came, he or she could either choose from a wrapped gift or take an opened gift from someone else.

I was number seven. My present was a framed black-and-white photo of a large tree surrounded by snow. Sitting on one of the branches was a brilliant red cardinal.

The evening ended around 10:00 p.m. As I got ready to leave, Bobbie stopped me. "Would you like to stay for a while? We can have a glass of wine and enjoy the fire."

I was grateful for her invitation. Staying for a drink and enjoying quality family time next to a roaring fire was better than facing the reality of going back to an empty house.

When I got home, I placed my gifts under the Christmas tree, put on Christmas music, and poured myself a glass of wine. I did not want the evening to end. *Why did the photographer change the color of the black-and-white cardinal to red in the picture?* I wondered as I gazed at my present. *Is there a special significance to a red cardinal?*

I searched the Internet and discovered that the symbolic sign of a red cardinal has been long embraced as the most notable spiritual messenger who has been sent from a loved one in heaven to watch over us.

Every day, I'd had mixed emotions about God, wondering where He was and how he could have allowed Tony to do such a terrible thing. In the past few weeks, I prayed many times, and it felt like God was nowhere to be found. But tonight, He appeared in the form of a red cardinal. Peace slipped over me, as I felt the presence of my guardian angels and God's loving hands around me.

The next day I woke up with great anticipation of flying to Florida in two days' time. To keep my mind off my empty home, I distracted myself with packing. The visual of my golf clubs, luggage on the floor, and the thought of being in warmer weather added to my excitement.

Later that afternoon, Jay called. "We arrived in Florida a few days ago. The weather is perfect. I'm calling to make sure you're still coming. I hope so. We are going to have so much fun."

"My bags are packed, and I am ready to go. I gave Denise my flight information."

"Great! We'll pick you up at the airport. Joe and Gail arrived today."

I was happy that I kept my plans in place to go to Florida. Jay and Denise and Joe and Gail were Tony's and my best friends. I looked forward to the comfort of my friends and sharing good times. We had all played golf together at the Brandywine Country Club in Wilmington, so playing golf was going to be the focus of our trip.

The six of us were inseparable as friends. In addition to playing golf and enjoying dinners, we also enjoyed movies and concerts together. Now this party of six was a party of five. I was no longer part of a couple; I was a fifth wheel. Although I was grateful for them keeping our New Year's plans in place, I also felt that it would be a matter of time before we would go our separate ways because of me being the odd man out.

The day I arrived we talked about our New Year's Eve plans. Everyone seemed excited. But I just couldn't share their enthusiasm. Just the thought of seeing all the couples kissing at the stroke of midnight while I stood alone made me feel sick to my stomach. I hated to put a damper on their celebration, but I also knew I needed to be honest.

"I'd like to stay home that night."

"Absolutely not," Jay said. "We already paid for you as our guest. New Year's would not be the same without you."

I knew they were trying to include me and make me feel better, and I appreciated it. Though I still really didn't treasure the idea of the evening, I agreed to go along.

New Year's Eve was upon us before we knew it, and that night we headed to the Palm Beach Polo & Country Club for a delicious meal. I tried to enjoy it, but I kept thinking about the stroke of midnight. *Maybe I could just excuse myself and go to the ladies' room during that time*, I thought.

"You know," Gail said. "We don't really need to stay here until midnight, do we?"

"Great," we all agreed, "let's head back to your place."

My friends must have realized how I would feel. Inwardly I sighed with relief.

We arrived back to Jay and Denise's home by 10:30 p.m., and we were all in bed by 11:00 p.m. Taking anxiety drugs mixed with alcohol helped me fall into a deep sleep.

The next night at dinner, we spoke about our amazing day. Out of the blue, Jay said, "Did you know that nine of the September 11 terrorists trained near Boca Raton? I can't begin to imagine how someone would make the choice to fly a suicide mission destroying the World Trade Center. And the first building attacked with anthrax is not too far from our house."

"It was definitely the worst day in everyone's lives, Joe said, then he looked quickly at me. "Let's talk about something else besides death and suicide." Everyone looked at me and agreed.

On January 1, 2002, the Homeland Security threat level was yellow. Our military stood ready 24/7 in anticipation of another attack.

While playing golf on New Year's Day, we noticed a pilot skywriting a welcome message in the new year. He wrote, "God Is Great," along with other similar messages two miles above the city. Given that we were only four months out from the terrorist attacks of September 11, 2001, people on the golf course were starting to panic as they wondered aloud whether this might be a warning preparing people for another terrorist attack. Many people even fled the course.

I felt nervous. "What should we do?" I turned to Denise. "Have you ever seen a plane skywriting before?"

"No, but let's wait here and ask Jay and Joe what to do." They were playing golf two holes behind us.

We stood off to the side and waited for them to arrive. But Jay didn't seem that bothered. "It's probably nothing. If there is a threat, we would hear a loud horn." Golfers know that it's standard protocol to sound a warning siren if there is a potential risk of lightning. They would also sound the warning siren in the case of an emergency.

The next day we read an article in the *Boca Raton Tribune,* which explained the confusion of the skywriting message. The article stated that a crop duster, Jerry Stevens from Boca Raton, took to the sky to write the message that God loves us and to encourage people to think about God and that love.

As I read the article, I felt that the pilot's skywriting was a message exclusively for me from God, and it brought me peace.

I returned home from Florida and immediately drove to my in-laws' house, as I had promised them. When I arrived, I noticed that my father-in-law's car was not in the driveway. I gave a sigh of relief. I walked into my mother-in-law's bedroom and found her sitting in a chair, crying and praying the rosary. She seemed startled, which was understandable since I had not called ahead to say I was coming.

"Hello, Mom. I just returned from Florida. I thought about you and Dad the entire time I was away. How are you feeling?" I knew it was a stupid question, but I was not sure what to say.

"Words cannot express how I am feeling. Your father and I cannot stop crying. We keep asking Jason questions about Anthony, but he will not give us any answers. I'm sure he knows more than what he is telling us. It feels like he is keeping us in the dark."

"I know exactly how you feel. I do not have a clue why Anthony killed himself. I'm going to start an investigation on my own to see if I can get some answers. I'll keep you posted."

My mother-in-law and I both started crying. I attempted to comfort her, but it was awkward as she sat in the chair. So I found myself sitting at her feet and holding her hands as we both cried. I kept my visit short so I would not upset her any more than I had and decided to leave before my father-in-law came home.

As I was leaving, I noticed Christine in the kitchen. "I will call you next week to see how everyone is doing. Maybe we can have dinner together."

"Okay," she replied simply.

I called Christine every day for a week and left messages for her to contact me. She never returned any of my calls.

As each day passed, I had hoped my grief would subside or at least lessen, but it didn't. When he was alive, Tony always called me twice a day and told me that he loved me. Now I stared at the phone that no longer rang, and my heart ached to hear those words from him once more.

But the worst was just not knowing the why. Why had he killed himself? Why had he purchased a gun, when he'd led me to believe he detested them? If he was depressed, why didn't he talk to me? I always felt that we had a good relationship. We never fought and rarely had any disagreements. Then my mind turned toward his family. Why were they treating me so poorly when I needed them the most? Why was Christine not returning my phone calls?

I couldn't keep living this way. It was destroying my sanity. So I called David. "Would you help me start a cold case investigation?" With his law enforcement experience, he'd know where to start looking for answers. I felt that I could not move forward until I put the past behind me.

To make matters worse, the grim reaper seemed to be working overtime that month. My closest neighbors living on the same floor were elderly. Within three weeks of each other, my next-door neighbor's husband died, followed by the husband of my neighbor across the hall. Three deaths on my floor within three weeks of one another. Grief was hitting us repeatedly and not letting us forget.

Before my next-door neighbor's husband died, I did not know her. I always kept to myself and worked many hours. I rarely saw any of my neighbors, because we were on different schedules. About six months after Tony's death, though, our paths crossed in the hallway. We began to talk, and Dorine invited me into her home.

I felt ashamed that she had lived next door to me for two years, and we had never met. A tiny, frail woman with short gray hair, Dorine reminded me of my mother—a little spunky, cursed a bit in a fun way, and loved vodka. I fell in love with her instantly, and she became my new best friend.

When I was sick, I always found a large container of chicken soup placed at my door. Every day I would knock on her door to make sure that she was okay, since she was in her late eighties and now lived by herself.

One day as we were chatting, she casually mentioned her great-niece Hallie. "Oh, you probably know her. She's Joe Biden's daughter-in-law. She's married to Beau."

"I don't know her personally, but I certainly know of her!" I said and laughed. Actually, I had known Hallie's parents for many years, though I did not know that she was Dorine's niece.

Living in Delaware, it was nearly impossible not to know some member of the Biden clan, especially because Joe Biden and his family always made it a point to be very visible and approachable.

"Ah yes," she said, laughing as well. "Everyone who lives in Delaware—especially here in Wilmington—knows there are only two degrees of separation regarding Joe Biden and his family."

"That's true." As a child, our family lived just five houses away from the Biden family. I rode the school bus with Joe's brother Jimmy. Years later, when I saw him, Jimmy reminded me that he kissed me on the school bus in the sixth grade.

One day about two weeks after I'd called David to ask him to help me do some investigating, I arrived home from some shopping to find Amy and David in my house.

"I didn't expect you, or I would have been here sooner," I told them, feeling surprised and suspicious.

"We have some information about Tony," David said, acting awkward and uncomfortable.

Really? What could they possibly know about Tony? I inhaled deeply. "I'm not sure that I'm ready to hear this."

David and Amy passed a glance between them.

"Mom, maybe you should sit down," Amy said gently.

My stomach tightened. What had they found out?

"What we're about to tell you . . . we've confirmed it, so it's true," Amy continued.

"Okay."

"Cheri," she said, referring to her stepmother, "works for an attorney who specializes in bankruptcies. A few days after Tony's death, she overheard a colleague talking about a friend of hers. The woman said that her boyfriend had committed suicide. Cheri thought, '*That's crazy!*' Weird that she heard about two deaths, both from gunshot wounds, within two days of each other. So Cheri started asking questions." Amy paused and looked again at David who nodded grimly.

"When Cheri asked the man's name, the woman told her, 'Tony Grillo.'"

I placed my hands over my eyes in disbelief and sat motionless. I felt as though someone had just punched me in the face.

Finally, I looked up. "Are you sure? What else did Cheri say?"

Amy said that when Cheri told the woman that Tony was married, she refused to believe it. The woman said that Tony had been a part of her girlfriend's family for more than five years and even vacationed with them."

"What?" I said.

"Mom, this woman has photos. Tony was part of their 'family' portrait," she said, using air quotes around *family*.

My eyes were open, but I did not see. *Could this be true?* Instead of giving me answers, they only gave me more questions.

Had I been so focused on building my fine jewelry and diamond business that I missed what was going on in my backyard? I never questioned Tony's loyalty and welcomed the extra time when he was away on "business" to make my own business successful.

And it had paid off. My greatest accomplishment was selling three diamonds in one day, with the total sales exceeding $100,000. Tony had been so proud of me that he sent me a dozen roses and took me out to dinner to celebrate that night. I'd worked so hard that year, my total sales as an independent jeweler were greater than Quality Automotive Parts' total sales.

But now what was so wonderful about those bragging rights? I'd succeeded in business, only to discover that my husband was investing his time and energy in another relationship and another woman's family?

I felt ashamed, humiliated. How could I not have known this?

Who even was *my husband, really?*

"I'm so sorry, Mom," Amy said, bringing my thoughts back to the present. She handed me a list that had several names written on it.

"What's this?" I looked down briefly at it and then back to Amy.

"Those are the names of several women Tony had affairs with."

I looked back down at it, now focusing more clearly on the names. I knew three of the women. One woman and her husband had even gone on a wine tour with us through Italy.

I began screaming and tossing anything that got in my way. A panic attack came on full-blown, making me shake uncontrollably. And then I got angry.

I picked up the phone and called two of the women I knew to let them know that I knew about their affairs with my husband. "How dare you!" I told each of them. "You disgust me. There are no words you can say that will be good enough for me to hear."

Each of them remained in stunned silence.

My anger followed with words of advice: "You may wish to have tests done for sexually transmitted diseases. Tony was having relationships with many other women while he was cheating on me with you."

I couldn't get my head around what he'd done. I'd been with him for sixteen years, married to him for thirteen, and I had no idea who this person was. I thought things like that only happened in the movies or to other people, but not to me.

After I heard about Tony's affairs, I called his daughter Melissa. I'm not sure why. I guess I wanted her to know that her father was not the man we all thought him to be.

Her husband, Jeffrey, answered the phone.

"I just heard some alarming news about Anthony. I just found out that he had been seeing many women at the time of his death. Am I the only person who did not know that he was unfaithful?"

He sighed quietly. "I found out about Anthony's affairs right after he died. I know that you stopped by to see Anthony's mother after returning from Florida and that you requested Christine to go out to dinner. I also know that you called her many times, and she has not returned your calls." He continued with a softer voice. "Don't expect anyone from the family to call you. They are putting you into the same category as the 'other women' in Anthony's life, and they are blaming you for his death. Also, the family heard a rumor that you found out about Anthony's affairs and were planning on leaving him."

I was stunned by his admission and what he was telling me about the family. "That statement is false. I was not planning to leave Anthony. I just found out about his affairs today."

The truth hit me like a solid block. I now understood why fifty-five members of Tony's family walked away from me, and I vowed never to talk to his family again.

You are never too old to set another goal or to dream a new dream.
—C. S. Lewis

CHAPTER 4

MY NEXT TRAUMATIC EVENTS

There are wounds that never show on the body that are deeper
and more hurtful than anything that bleeds.
—Laurell K. Hamilton, **Mistral's Kiss**

A fter I hung up the phone with one of Tony's lovers, I began to reflect on the conversations I'd had with her and another woman. I'd told them both, "You may wish to have tests done for sexually transmitted diseases. Tony was having relationships with *many* other women while he was cheating on me with you."

Oh no, I thought as the heavy weight of realization dropped onto me. *I have to be tested too!* My breathing came fast and panicked. "I could have a STD!" I yelled, staring up at my daughter, who should never have to hear those words from her mother.

"Mom, I feel so sorry for you. There are no words I can say. I know you are outraged. Right now, though, you need to calm down." Amy's voice was stern. "It's too late to do anything about the situation tonight. It's best to relax and call your doctor in the morning."

I knew she was right, but it was easier said than done to calm down and relax, as she'd commanded. "I need to take some anxiety medication and go to bed. Please don't tell anyone about our conversation. I'm embarrassed for anyone to know."

"Of course," Amy said, now more kindly. "Call me tomorrow and let me know when you will see the doctor. Would you like me to go with you?"

As much as I wanted her support through this, I couldn't ask her to listen in on the intimate details of her mother's sex life. I shook my head. "Thanks, but I've got this. You have done so much for me already. I think it would be best for you to spend quality time with Mackenzie."

Before leaving my house, Amy and I cried in each other's arms for quite some time. She wanted to stay with me, but she needed to be with Mackenzie and David. They had only been parents for six months, and they were dealing with many challenges on their own.

"Call me if you need anything or just want to talk," she said as she and David got ready to leave.

"I'm really sorry that we had to give you this news," David said.

"I know. But I'd rather have heard it from you two than somebody else."

Even though I took sleeping pills and anxiety medication, and drank a vodka gimlet, I did not sleep well that night and awoke early the next morning. I took a long hot shower, then drank coffee while I put on makeup and fixed my hair. My stomach was too upset to eat anything.

At precisely 9:00 a.m., I called my doctor's office and let the scheduler know I needed to see him today.

"I am very sorry, but the doctor doesn't have any openings today. He can see you tomorrow at 4:30 p.m. Would that be okay?"

"Absolutely not. I need to see Dr. Krasner today. Please check with him now. I'm certain he will see me."

She paused for a moment. "I'm sorry, he's with a patient. May I put you on hold, or would you like me to call you back?"

I started to sob. "Please put me on hold." I waited for more than ten minutes and with each passing minute began hyperventilating more uncontrollably.

When I didn't think I could wait another minute, my doctor's voice came on the line. "Please come into my office at noon. We can talk when you come in, okay?"

"Thank You, God," I said as soon as I hung up. A noon appointment would give me a chance to relax and compose myself mentally and physically. I looked in the mirror. *There's that disheveled woman looking back at me again. When is she going to go away?*

I arrived at my doctor's office at 11:45 a.m. After signing in, the receptionist handed me paperwork to complete, since it was a new year and they wanted to update their records.

I sat in the waiting room and began to answer the questions. After entering my name and contact information, I looked at the next line. "Marital Status: Single, Married, Divorced, Widowed." My heart sank into my stomach. Today was the first time I'd had to acknowledge that I was a widow, and I began to cry. I couldn't circle the word.

Eventually a nurse escorted me to an examination room where I waited for my doctor. Within a few minutes, the door opened. "Janet, I am so sorry for your loss," he said. He lifted me from the chair and hugged me as a fresh wave of tears came.

After I wiped my eyes with a tissue, I breathed in deeply and began to admit the horrifying news and worries. "I'm here because I found out that my husband was unfaithful to me and was involved with many women at the time of his death."

He sighed heavily with a sound of deep compassion. "I'm sorry to hear this." He confirmed that I needed blood work to determine if I had any sexually transmitted diseases and gave me a prescription to take to the laboratory.

I left his office and sat crying in my car for more than an hour, unable to summon up the strength or courage to take on one more task for the day. I was fragile and too embarrassed to ask anyone for help. As soon as I drove home, I took two anxiety pills and sat motionless for the rest of the day.

A thousand thoughts went through my mind. *I am a widow. My husband committed suicide in a veterans' cemetery. Tony's family walked away from me. My husband was unfaithful our entire marriage and even had a five-year relationship with one woman and several relationships with women I know. Now I have to have blood work done to determine if I have any STDs.*

I closed my eyes. *Please, God, take my hand and never let me go. I cannot face another day on my own. I am scared and feel all alone.*

As though in answer to my prayer, a thought came to my mind to spend some time with God and read the Bible. But I was unsure where to begin. I once heard that if we open the Bible to what we think is a random page, in reality, it's actually God directing us to the passages we need in that moment.

I opened the Bible and looked down to see the book of Romans 8. I read verses 38-39: "I am convinced that neither death nor life, neither angels nor demons, neither the present nor the future, nor any powers, neither height nor depth, nor anything else in all creation, will be able to separate us from the love of God that is in Christ Jesus our Lord." God was reminding me that no matter how bad life gets, He will not stop loving me. In my life I will have things go right and I will have things go wrong, but God's love will be the steadfast thing I can count on. It will never end. *That truth should be one of the most important sources of joy in my life*, I realized.

I grabbed a journal and started writing in it to collect my thoughts and document events and conversations that I'd had throughout the years with Tony. One of the events I remembered happened five years previously. I experienced a burning sensation when I went to the bathroom. I thought it was merely a bladder infection, so I drank much cranberry juice and scheduled an appointment with a urologist. That burning sensation turned out to be a severe case of chlamydia. It was so intense that the urologist admitted me to the hospital and began treating me with intravenous antibiotics. He explained that I could only have contracted it through intercourse.

As I had been 100 percent faithful to my husband and knew I was not responsible for my STD, I called Tony and told him the situation. "The urologist said that I could only contract this through sexual intercourse. Have you been unfaithful to me?"

"Absolutely not!" he said, his voice sounding offended. "You must have gotten it from a toilet seat." He vehemently insisted that he had been faithful and then questioned my faithfulness. And somehow he convinced me that the doctor was wrong, that it must have, indeed, been a toilet seat transmission.

For the next two days while I suffered alone in the hospital, Tony visited his parents at their beach house in Avalon, New Jersey, but never once stepped a foot in my hospital room. He didn't even show up to take me home after I was discharged.

A day later, he finally returned home. I thought it best to talk about my infection, since the toilet seat transmission idea just didn't sound right. "Tony, we have to talk about this. I have been completely faithful to you. But my doctor insists that I could only get the disease from another person."

His face went red. "The doctors are crazy," he said angrily. "If you got infected, it did not come from me."

We never spoke about the incident again. Worse was that he refused to touch me for months, making me feel worthless. I thought this was his way of punishing me. But now as I wrote the story in my journal, I sensed that he knew he was the one at fault and abstained from having sex because he did not want to take the chance of infecting me again.

The next day I decided to drive to the neighboring state of Pennsylvania for my tests. I feared that I would see someone I knew and did not want to add additional stress to my day. When I arrived at the diagnostics lab, I handed the technician the test order from my doctor. He had checked every box for all nine tests—HIV type 1, HIV type 2, chlamydia, gonorrhea, syphilis, herpes, and hepatitis A, B, and C.

As I watched the phlebotomist draw nine vials of blood, I felt mortified. Then I drove home, feeling frightened and dirty. At home, I took off my clothes and wanted to burn them.

For the next ten days as I waited for my test results, I increased my anxiety medication and alcohol intake. I was a basket case.

"What did I do to deserve this?" I shouted at God. "I'm a good person." Just then I remembered. Tony and I had met and gotten involved with each other eighteen years before when we were both married to other people. I felt that this STD I now possibly had was God's way of punishing me for my sins, so I smeared His name up one side and down the other—even though I knew it was Tony's fault, not God's. I guess I just needed someone to blame. I defiantly hated the only One who could help and heal me. Exhaustion got the best of me as I cried myself to sleep.

I awoke in the middle of the night choking. The smell of vomit on my breath disgusted me, though I was too weak to do anything about it. *I deserve whatever punishment God has in store for me.*

After several fitful hours, I fell asleep again and woke up in the morning to find my Bible laying in bed next to me. *That's strange. I don't remember bringing it to bed.* I thought it was a silent sign from God that I needed to open my Bible just one more time.

I read several passages. One that made a great impression on me was Proverbs 3:5-6: "Trust in the Lord with all your heart and lean not on your own understanding; in all your ways submit to Him, and He will make your paths straight." One thing I knew for sure was that I did not have any understanding of what was happening in my life. I knew I would *have* to trust Him.

Then I turned to my favorite passage, Jeremiah 29:11: "'I know the plans I have for you,' declares the Lord, 'plans to prosper you and not to harm you, plans to give you hope and a future.'" I remembered a quote I'd read once that corresponded with this verse: "Don't worry about tomorrow, God is already there." That had helped me get through many struggles. Anytime I felt uncertain about my future, I would consistently chant in my mind, *Don't worry about tomorrow, God is already there.* It always helped remove worries from my mind.

Now the more I read the Bible, the more I realized, *Sometimes God allows us to sin, being fully aware of how He's going to use the experience.* I knew that did not excuse my sins. But I did know that no matter what the sin, God was willing to forgive it.

I spent the next week barely leaving my bedroom. Occasionally I would visit my office to get my mind off the inevitable, but too many thoughts cluttered my head. Most days, I found myself returning to my bedroom and closing the door behind me. It was my safe place.

A few days later, my doctor's office called to schedule an appointment for the next day to discuss my blood test results. The twenty-four-hour waiting period seemed like twenty-four days. Once I received the phone call, I started having anxiety attacks, where I imagined horrible possibilities. The worst was yet to come, I believed.

The next morning, I felt sick to my stomach. I started to brush my teeth and felt myself vomiting. I quickly ran to the toilet and hugged the bowl for a long time as I cried and wondered where I was going to find the strength to move. As the queasiness waned, I lay on the bathroom floor motionless for a long time.

Eventually I got back up and slowly started to get ready. I looked at the clock and realized that I would be late, if I did not pick up my pace. I brushed my teeth, took a shower, and got dressed, feeling as though I were getting dressed for my funeral. I'd run out of time to style my hair and apply makeup. I felt horrible and no longer cared if my appearance represented the same.

I waited patiently and impatiently in the exam room, as I prepared for my death sentence. For a split second, I thought suicide would be the only way to make my pain go away. The anxiety of the unknown was more than I could bear.

The door opened slowly as my doctor and his assistant walked in. He clutched two file folders. One appeared more like an encyclopedia. We spoke no words. But just as the previous time, he lifted me from my chair, hugged me, and started to cry.

He was crying so hard that he was unable to speak, which made me and his assistant also cry. I wanted to run out of his office and disappear. In that split second, I gave myself a month or two to live and wondered how I would survive. As soon as he let me go, I collapsed back into my chair, though still holding his hands.

"All of your tests are negative," he said, his voice quivering. "Ever since I requested the tests, I've been praying for you. I also prayed for myself and asked God for strength and courage. But even with prayer, I didn't know where I was going to find the strength to tell you if Tony had infected you with an STD."

Though my body became weak with exhaustion, hard tears now came. I began to wheeze from a self-induced asthma attack. His assistant quickly exited to get me an inhaler to control my breathing.

The doctor sat opposite me. "Janet, I treated Tony four times for sexually transmitted diseases in ten years. One case was so severe that he insisted on paying cash for his visit and did not want any record written into his chart."

My jaw dropped. I was so stunned, I wasn't sure what to feel any longer.

He told me that Tony also visited the office on many other occasions, thinking that he had STDs, though they turned out negative. Yet even with so many disease scares, Tony continued to enlist other women's services, including prostitutes, I would learn later.

Tony hurt me when he died, and now he's hurting me from his grave. Will this pain ever end? God, where are You when I need You the most?

My doctor gave me a prescription for medication to help me sleep and to cope with anxiety attacks. He also gave me a prescription to see a psychologist, which I was grateful for, since I'd been on an emotional and physical roller coaster with no signs of hope, let alone any signs of recovery. I desperately needed to talk to someone.

I immediately called for an appointment, and couldn't get in to see the psychologist, Dr. Margaret Todd, until the following week.

While I waited for the week to pass, I fell into a state of depression. Even though I was taking sleeping pills and anxiety medication, I had challenges falling asleep. I lost my appetite, my energy level was shallow, my self-esteem was low, I had difficulty concentrating, I cried excessively, and I felt hopeless. I lacked confidence in myself and felt unlovable, awkward, and incompetent.

It had been bad enough that my husband had committed suicide, but he'd done so many other things to hurt me. *Why?* I kept asking myself. I thought that the only way to rid myself of the pain was to die by suicide. Even though the thought did not stay with me for very long, the idea kept entering my mind.

The day for my appointment arrived and I was pleasantly surprised when I entered the psychologist's office. The soft blue walls immediately calmed my nerves, and I felt peaceful. Knowing that help was behind a closed door relaxed my anxiety and slowed my heart rate.

Dr. Todd came out of her office and introduced herself. She was nothing like I expected. Standing only at about 5'2", she look as if she weighed two hundred pounds. She wore no makeup, and her bleached-blonde hair was pulled into a ponytail. Her outfit appeared to be put on out of convenience with no thought of making a fashion statement.

Immediately I felt more relaxed. *I think this is someone I can trust.*

She reached out her hand and gave me a firm handshake.

As we stepped into her office, I was struck by the soothing green color she'd chosen for the walls and the many plants displayed around the room.

"How are you feeling today? Are you taking any medication to help you cope with your stress?"

"I was a little nervous about today's visit, because I did not know what to expect." Then I gave her a list of the medications I was taking, including Ambien, which the doctor had recently prescribed to help me sleep.

"Be very careful when taking Ambien. It can be addicting and can have terrible side effects."

I promised I would.

She began to ask about my family and my support system. "Is your family supporting you in this process? How is your husband's family toward you? Are they supportive?"

I sat frozen for a moment and bit the inside of my cheek before I replied. "My daughter, my son-in-law, and my sisters and their families have been very supportive. They invite me to visit often. Lately, I have declined many of their invitations, though, because honestly, I would prefer to stay home in my bedroom. When I venture outside of my family, I discover people pointing fingers at me and whispering behind my back. It makes me want to crawl into a hole and die."

She quietly listened.

"Regarding my husband's family," I continued, "they walked away from me shortly after my husband's death."

"Your husband was a sick man and possibly suffered from depression. We may never know the exact reason why he killed himself."

"My family feels that my husband's family knows the secrets of his betrayals and the judgment for his death. They thought that his family turned their backs on me to keep the secrets within the family."

She smiled sadly. "A true full-blooded Italian family."

"In hindsight, I feel many people knew of my husband's wayward life and chose not to make me aware of the situation. They knew that I would end my marriage immediately. Some have even feared for my safety. I've felt overwhelmed with peoples' suspicions and truths. They knew my husband better than I did."

Confessing that made me think, *Why do some people fear for my safety? What could others possibly know that they have not already shared with me?* I wondered again about the suspicious-looking men at my husband's viewing who wore trench coats, dripped in gold chains, and wore dark sunglasses.

Dr. Todd interrupted my thoughts. "You have extensive issues to work through in addition to your husband and the circumstances around his death. It will take some time; your healing will not happen overnight. It may take months or even years, but I promise you that you will get through this."

As she spoke into my life, I felt as though God was holding me in the palm of His hands when I was too weak to walk and too fragile to stand on my own. *Thank You for such safe harbor*, I prayed.

Later that week I received a bill in the mail for the cemetery plot I'd purchased at Saint Joseph's on the Brandywine in Greenville, Delaware, a suburb of Wilmington. I bought a burial plot for two and paid for one-half. I planned to pay for my resting place after I collected the insurance money.

Within a month after Tony's death, I collected copies of his insurance policies and a copy of the company's agreement regarding any corporate family member's death. I was pleased to see that financially I would be just fine. But when I contacted the insurance company, they informed me that Tony's two daughters had received the premium checks from his policy. I was bewildered and asked why, since I had a copy of the insurance policy that named me as the beneficiary.

"I'm sorry, Mrs. Grillo. Our paperwork indicates that Tony's daughters are the beneficiaries."

I hung up the phone and got to work researching what had happened. I soon discovered that the insurance agent who wrote the policy redirected the funds to Tony's daughters. When I contacted my attorney about it, he suggested that I hire a second attorney who specialized in wills and probates. "Looks like the insurance agent illegally transferred the funds," he told me.

The insurance agent was a personal friend of Tony's and even collaborated with him on some business deals. Every week they had lunch together with a man who owned several large car dealerships in many states. I never understood why Tony collaborated on business ventures with this man. When I asked, he just said, "Our business is complicated. You wouldn't understand." Since he never gave me a direct answer, I stopped asking questions.

Let the games begin, I thought. My second attorney found out the name of the daughters' attorney. She was one of the most expensive in the city where they lived. Their attorney argued that I had signed a prenuptial agreement and was not entitled to the money. There was nothing in the prenup that stated or allowed for any discrepancy.

Bottom line, federal laws govern prenuptial agreements, not state laws. I won my case after much deliberation, though it cost me $25,000 to settle out of court.

I was naïve to think that, as Tony's wife, I would be treated fairly. Getting what I deserved would take me much time and money, so I knew I needed to put on my big girl pants and fight for everything— especially the assets that were legally mine.

A few days later, I received a phone call from my attorney with more bad news. One of Tony's family members terminated my health insurance policy without notification. According to my attorney, his actions were chargeable as a federal offense. I didn't have the energy to fight every battle, so I had to choose the more important ones. I chose not to pursue the matter and felt it best to pay for my health insurance.

My attorney fees were increasing minute by minute. If I filed charges against my husband's family, my attorney fees would dramatically increase. At that point, the fees exceeded $100,000.

Not long after, another family member, with whom my husband owned a building that they'd purchased twenty years before as part of the company grounds, convinced me that the property was worth nothing by itself. After deliberating with my attorney, we agreed on a $25,000 settlement.

Six months later, he sold the building for more than $500,000. My share would have been a $250,000. I was outraged. At that point, however, there was nothing I could do. I learned the hard way not to trust anything and to dissect and question every piece of paperwork in my possession.

A few weeks later, a cousin dropped off a box of items from Tony's office and left it with the concierge at my building. The package included his wallet with credit cards, his checkbook registers for the past five years, and fiction books.

I thought that was strange. I never saw Tony read a book except for one he'd read on the airplane when he took me to Paris to celebrate my fiftieth birthday. I remember Tony telling me that he purchased the book at the airport. That was a lie.

Someone cut off the price tag. Most often, it signifies that the book was a gift. Upon closer inspection, I discovered that the main character's name was Laura. I also learned that one of the women Tony was having an affair with was named Laura. But Laura was *not* the name of the woman he'd had a five-year relationship with.

This is crazy! Are there any *women in Delaware my husband did not have a relationship with? Maybe I should use* that *list. It might be a shorter one to work with!*

Enclosed in Tony's wallet I found his platinum American Express card. I asked my attorney to investigate the American Express account. I was going to use the information as a starting point for my investigation.

One would naturally assume that since my husband was president of the family-owned business, he would be the primary cardholder. That was not the case. My attorney discovered that the primary cardholder was someone with a different name, other than Grillo.

"Whose name is on it?" I asked.

"Unfortunately, for legal reasons, I cannot give you the name. I can only tell you that the last name is not Grillo."

Perhaps his financial advisor/insurance agent was the primary, I thought. *He's such a sly fox with many connections.*

I remembered seeing him at Tony's viewing. He talked to the group of men who wore the long trench coats. They all gathered together in a corner in the back of the viewing room. Although I'm sure they intended to go unnoticed, they stood out prominently and suspiciously.

That's when everything came crashing in on me. *Was Tony part of the mafia? Were the men at the viewing present to confirm that Tony was dead?* I could feel my heart begin to race and I told myself to calm down. *You're just being paranoid, Janet.* Even though I suspected that he had shady dealings, and thought many of them could have been mafia related, I made myself dismiss the thought. It was too terrifying.

My attorney found out that someone opened the American Express account in 1990. We got married in 1988. I wondered if Tony had been involved in something illegal many years before we got married or did he get involved shortly afterward? Nothing made sense to me.

I thought back to something Tony told me a month before he died—that his cousin had requested a meeting with him to discuss the accounting books.

I'm not sure why he told me about the upcoming meeting. I am certain Tony embezzled money from the company to support his extramarital affairs. Perhaps his cousin had found proof to confront him.

What exactly was going on? What exactly was Tony's involved in? And worse, was Tony's death really a suicide? Perhaps it was an assisted suicide? Or a suggested one?

I wondered if his cousin had told him that he would take legal actions against him, and in Tony's eyes, death seemed easier than shaming himself and his family. I did not feel that his cousin would suggest that Tony end his life—that was ultimately Tony's decision, or was it? Maybe the decision was made for him by someone other than a family member?

I began thinking more seriously about the mafia idea. I knew Italians had a reputation for being connected to organized crime and for cheating on their wives. By the 1950s, the mafia had become the preeminent organized-crime network in the United States. Their underworld activities ranged from loan-sharking to prostitution.

Tony's family's company had more than one hundred clients nationally and internationally, and Tony had been responsible for all of the accounts except for one. Zachary was responsible for that one—and it was in Philadelphia, a hub of the mafia, I knew. *My best guess is that they were fencing stolen automotive parts.*

Now I became more determined than ever to find out why my husband was dead, and I felt like one of the first places to start was at with Tony's cell phone company. I enlisted Amy and David's assistance. I needed to find closure before I could move forward with my life.

The following Monday, armed with the manager's name, the three of us met at the Nextel store at the Foulkstone Plaza in Wilmington at 10:00 a.m. We decided that I would do all the talking and we rehearsed what I would say.

We entered the store and sought out the manager.

"Is there a room where we can talk in private?" I said. "My husband died mysteriously, and I need to view his cell phone records. I feel that viewing the records may answer many of my questions." I explained that my husband died tragically, and I did not know if his death was a suicide, assisted suicide, suggested suicide, or murder. I added murder to have a significant effect on my request. I thought adding suspense and drama would create a more sympathetic response.

"I have to search our records and print them out," she said. "It may take fifteen to twenty minutes."

As she left the room, I turned to Amy and David. "I feel very optimistic and can hardly wait to see the bills."

More than one hour passed, and we were still waiting for the manager to return. We thought it best not to rush her and appreciated her attention to start my investigation, but still it seemed a long time to wait.

Finally, she returned to the room, holding a stack of papers. She handed me a cell phone.

I looked at her, feeling confused with her gesture.

"The phone is registered to Quality Automotive Parts. Your name is not on the contract. I needed permission to give you the information, so I called your husband's company."

I put the phone to my ear and was surprised to hear Zachary's voice.

"What are you doing?" he asked.

"I am trying to find out information about why my husband killed himself."

"You have no authorization to look at any paperwork from our company," he said, his voice booming.

"My husband is dead," I yelled into the phone. "And I need to know why. The phone records may give me some information to uncover why he killed himself."

"I *do not* want you to call our customers and ask questions. Our customers may think that we are going to file for bankruptcy."

"The company does not have any customers in Delaware. I am only interested in the local phone numbers." Honestly, I knew three of the women Tony was having affairs with. I wondered if there were more women on the list whom I knew. I wondered if women I considered to be close friends had cheated with him.

"This is going to get very ugly, isn't it?"

I decided that I'd had enough of his verbal abuse and disconnected the call. There was no compassion for a grieving widow! I stormed out of the phone company, with Amy and David following. We stood by the car, talking about not obtaining the phone records and about Zachary's verbal abuse.

Where do I go from here? How am I going to start my investigation without phone records?

As we stood talking, David received a phone call. "It's Zachary."

After David answer, Zachary's voice was so loud, I could hear him. "What is Janet doing?"

"Janet is aware that there were many other women in Tony's life," David answered calmly. The phone records will start the process of her finding closure."

I could not imagine how my husband hid his wayward life from me. He was clearly very good at what he did—lying, cheating, and stealing. I hated myself for living my married life with my eyes closed.

After David hung up with Zachary, he looked at me sternly. "The company must be hiding something. There would be no reason to protect the other women."

"Mom, you need to stop investigating," Amy pled with me. "Everywhere you turn, it appears that Tony's family is lying to cover up something. There is a conspiracy going on."

I thought that situations like that only happened in the movies.

As much as I wanted to close the door and walk away from everything, I could not. The anger I held in my body was destroying me one day at a time. Many days I felt too weak to get out of bed. My anxiety attacks were getting worse every day, even though I was taking medication for stress. My whole life was crashing before me, and I did not know what to do.

One day I scheduled to drop paperwork off at my attorney's office. When I woke up that morning, I found that my right eye was completely swollen shut, and a bloody, green discharge was seeping from it. I wore contacts, and it felt like a contact lodged under my eyelid. *Did I forget to remove it last night?* The pain was unbearable. My face was numb. I wondered if I had a stroke.

Fortunately, the hospital was only one mile away. I did not call anyone to assist me because I didn't want to delay getting there. I stumbled into the emergency waiting room, holding an ice pack on my eye. After signing in and finding a seat in the corner of the waiting room, I buried my face into the ice pack and prayed, *Please, God, help me now. I am scared. I don't know if I can make it through this day.*

As soon as I'd prayed, I immediately felt an unexplainable peace come over me.

Is God here with me? Is He holding my hand and caressing my broken body? All I knew was that I was a basket case when I walked into the room, and all of a sudden, I was no longer scared, and I did not feel alone.

The emergency room doctor confirmed that I had an ulcer on the cornea of my eye. He did not, however, find a contact lodged under my eyelid.

"What can cause an infection like this?"

"People usually develop a corneal ulcer by some type of trauma, which allows bacteria to enter the cornea," he explained. "The invasion can cause an infection with inflammation. Stress and a weakened immune system can also cause an infection."

"How long will it take before it gets better?"

"Because this is an open sore on the cornea of your eye, it could take two to three weeks to heal. I'm going to give you a prescription for eye drops. However, you must make an appointment to see your eye doctor immediately."

I did as he commanded and scheduled an appointment for the following day at 2:00 p.m. I had to ask Amy to drive me, since the doctor was going to put eye drops in and I wouldn't be able to see.

The ophthalmologist took one look at my eye and nodded. "That's the correct diagnosis. I have treated many corneal ulcers. Your infection is one of the most severe I've seen. It's good that you came in right away. Otherwise, you could lose the vision in that eye."

I may go blind in my right eye? I couldn't believe this was happening to me!

"Because the ulceration is in the central cornea, the condition will take longer to heal," he said. "Your vision may be permanently reduced due to scarring. I want to prepare you for the inevitable. Permanent damage and vision loss may occur, even with us treating it early."

I cannot believe all the things that I've had to endure these past two months. Now there's a possibility that I may lose my eyesight!

The doctor gave me a prescription for eye drops and instructed me to stay in bed and watch little to no television. "I don't want you to overstress your eye." He scheduled a follow-up appointment for seven days later.

Each day I obediently used the eye drops and limited my television viewing, but my eye only continued to get worse instead of better. I was beside myself. I was sure that constant crying hindered my healing.

Now when I looked into the mirror and saw that disheveled-looking woman staring back at me, this time she looked like a cyclops. *What am I going to do?* Then my thought turned toward God. *My God, my God, why have You forsaken me?* Where was He in all of this? Did He care? Did He even exist?

Many years before, someone had introduced me to a network marketing company called Nikken, well known for their magnetic therapy. Nikken had introduced the PiMag water system, which turned regular tap water into PiWater, an alkaline and mineralized water, which they call "living water." I had one, so I decided to flush my eye with it several times a day.

Soon my eye began feeling better. When I returned to the eye doctor one week later, he took one look at my eye and leaned back in surprise. "I cannot believe what I'm seeing! I have never seen a corneal ulcer heal so quickly!" He examined it again. "And there is no scarring."

I told him my secret cure. "I rinsed my eye four times a day with the PiWater."

"I'm glad you thought to use it. I have never seen an eye with a corneal ulcer restored to new. The infection goes away, but there are always signs of scarring left behind. Washing your eye that way saved your vision and prevented permanent scarring."

For the first time in a very long time, I found hope. It was the only good news I'd heard in the two months since my husband's death. And although I felt that my prayers to God were falling on deaf ears, I continued to pray.

I continued because I had nowhere else to turn for help. I continued because I knew I did not have the courage or strength to attempt to repair myself independently.

I continued to pray to God because my heart told me not to worry about tomorrow; God was already there.

Trauma is a fact of life. It does not, however, have to be a life sentence.

—Peter A. Levine

CHAPTER 5

DISCOVERING I STILL HAD MUCH TO BE GRATEFUL FOR

You begin saving the world by saving one person at a time;
all else is grandiose romanticism or politics.
—Charles Bukowski

After months of seeing my psychiatrist, she realized that I was not making much progress with my healing process. Every time I tried to put the past behind me, members of Tony's family stirred the pot, refusing to sign off on financial matters. And I found out more about my husband's mystery life, not to mention more ladies of the evening were surfacing.

Although Dr. Todd kept focusing on the positives, I struggled not to focus on the negatives. She decided to take a different approach to help me gain more confidence in myself and to raise my self-esteem. "Helping other people is one way to take the focus off of ourselves," she said. "Helping others can save ourselves."

I nodded. "I've often heard that helping one person might not change the world, but it could change the world for one person."

"Can you think of a time when you helped someone or made a difference in someone's world?"

I shifted in my seat and began to smile. "I can think of five people I've had the opportunity to save or help save."

"Other than medical professionals, most people have not even saved one life. Your heroic efforts helped form you into the person you are today. Tell me about those instances."

I thought back over each time.

In 1973, I saved a boy from a house fire while visiting my sister Diane and her husband, Bill, in Germany. Bill served in the Air Force and was stationed at the Ramstein Air Base—Ramstein-Miesenbach.

While I was there, we attended a Fasching Celebration—a feasting time with frivolity, parades, parties, and people wearing masks and costumes to celebrate before the austerity of Lent. We had a wonderful time and at the stroke of midnight, we drove home. As we passed through a town called Weilerbach, we saw a large house engulfed in flames. We drove to the nearest phone booth to call the fire department, but we could not read the instructions written in German.

While my sister remained at the phone booth looking for a way to seek help, Bill and I ran to the burning house. We managed to break down one door and yelled in desperation for anyone to answer, hoping that if anyone was sleeping, our yells would awaken them. A man and his German Shepherd ran down the steps to safety. The fire was so intense that the stairway collapsed just as they exited the house into the below-freezing cold air.

The man ran out of one doorway and quickly into another portal. Shortly after, the charred man stood in the door's entrance carrying an older woman's body. He lay her on the concrete ground and quickly returned inside to rescue more people.

Bill and I looked at each other, uncertain what to do. We thought that if he recovered anyone else, everyone would freeze to death instead of dying in a fire. I ran across the street to get some blankets and ask the people to call the fire department."

A young woman answered the door only to find a hysterical woman screaming at the top of her lungs, asking her to call the fire department. "Please help," I told her, crying uncontrollably and pointing to the house on fire. We need blankets!"

The woman started crying too. She knew there was an emergency, but she did not know how to help because she didn't speak English.

The rescued people are wearing nightclothes in ten-degree tempera-tures, and she does not speak English. "I need blankets, cover, wool!"

"Ah, wool!" she said and quickly turned to get blankets.

I returned to the house and placed a blanket over the woman, only to learn that she was dead. I looked up to see the charred man standing in the doorway holding the body of a young boy dressed only in his white-brief underwear.

Bill and I grabbed the boy and lay him on the ground. By this time, many people had gathered and stood over his body, though none offered to assist.

I did not see the second blanket, so I ripped off my coat and covered the boy with it.

"Diane, get the car!" I yelled. "We have to get him to a hospital."

Within minutes, Diane drove the car onto the driveway. Bill placed the boy in the backseat, I scooted in next to him, and we headed to the air force base.

I checked to see if he was breathing, and he was not. I banged on his chest and gave him mouth-to-mouth resuscitation. Life slowly reentered his body.

We arrived at the military base twenty minutes later. The soldier at the gate gave us passage to the infirmary and called ahead to alert the doctors. Once we arrived, we got out of the way and let the doctors take over.

I learned later that the boy's parents felt my actions of saving their son's life was like him being reborn. They buried their grandmother and, a few days later, awarded me a 22-karat gold coin.

"You are a hero!" Dr. Todd said after I told her that story. "You saved the boy's life by giving him mouth-to-mouth resuscitation. One thing no one can ever take away from you is the feeling that you had when you helped save the boy and the amazing feeling you get every time you tell your story. Your heroic efforts changed the world for more than one person. You changed the world for the young boy, his family, and his future family."

Helping others can indeed be a cure, not only for those in need but also for restoring someone's soul, in addition to leaving a wonderful legacy behind, I realized.

"Are the rest of your life-saving stories as exciting as the last one?"

I smiled. "All are very exciting, except for the one where I saved a man's life from choking."

A sales representative stopped by my jewelry office to show me a new line of diamond jewelry. He took a piece of candy from my candy bowl and popped it into his mouth. But just as he did, he started to sneeze, and the candy lodged in his throat. He began to choke and gasped for air. I quickly put my arms around his body and gave him the Heimlich Maneuver. The candy immediately dislodged onto the floor. "The funny part is that I don't even remember his name," I said.

"It's amazing that you consider it a small action and even forgot his name," Dr. Todd said. "I assure you he will always remember the action you took to save his life, and he will never forget you. Okay, I am eager to hear your third story."

"Thinking back, I remember this story having a happy ending, but I also remember my husband's constant negativity over it, because I helped someone I did not know."

In 1988, I read a newspaper article in the *Wilmington News Journal* about a young, local boy named Bobby Fanny. He entered a skateboard competition in Philadelphia and was injured when he fell off his skateboard. Since he was not wearing a helmet, when he crashed his head onto the concrete, it caused catastrophic brain damage. Nerve damage in both of his legs was also severe. His brain was swelling rapidly. His doctor put him into a medically induced coma.

Bobby was one of the best skateboarders in his field and hoped to score high that day. As a teenager, his dream was to become a professional skateboarding champion.

The article was published to tell Bobby's story and to emphasize the importance of wearing a helmet. Doctors stated that Bobby had no hope for recovery, but that if he did live, he would be in a vegetative state for the rest of his life.

The year prior, I had become a representative for a company called Nikken. They are known for harnessing the energy in our natural environment and delivering it through life-enhancing technologies and products, such as through using magnetism. Nikken harnessed the energy in magnets of many different sizes and strengths and called it Magnetic Equalizing Technology. Applying the magnets on the body for extensive lengths of time will help the body restore to new.

As I read the newspaper article, my heart broke, thinking about Bobby's condition and his family's emotional state. I researched the family and phone number. But just as I was starting to call, my husband walked into the room.

"What are you doing?" he said.

When I explained that I was going to offer magnets to help Bobby, Tony replied with anger, "This child is none of your business, and you are crazy to think that the magnets will help." He demanded that I forget what I read and he motioned for me to hang up the phone.

But I couldn't. I knew I needed to share the information I'd learned with his parents. I could not live with myself if I didn't. After Tony left for work that day, I called Bobby's parents, introduced myself to his mother, and explained the reason for my call.

I suggested that they tape magnets around their son's head and on his lower back and place magnetic insoles in his socks. I proceeded to tell her that I did not want any money for the products. The gesture was purely from my heart.

The products cost me $300, yet I didn't share the dollar value.

Bobby's mother listened and then said, "Let me discuss our call and the magnets with my husband. I will call you tomorrow."

The next day as promised, she called at 3:00 p.m. "I am very sorry. I spoke with my husband, and he is outraged that you called. He said absolutely not."

"Please accept my offer," I told her. "If there is a 1 percent chance of saving your son's life, I would love to be the one who helped."

Against her husband's advice, Bobby's mother allowed me to give them the products. With the help of veteran Nikken representatives, I instructed the quantity and position of the magnets.

Bobby wore them 24/7 except when he was bathing or having therapy in a pool. Four weeks later, Bobby had significant improvement and returned home.

After a month, I called Bobby's mother to check in. She told me that he was doing well, but not great.

"The best thing to do is expose his body to more magnets," I said. "The greater the injury, the more magnets are needed to help the body realign itself. He needs to sleep on a mattress with magnets."

The wholesale cost of the mattress pad was $500. I was not in a financial position to give it to Bobby, and his parents were not in a financial place to pay because of their medical bills. We set up an arrangement for me to purchase it and for them to repay me in installments over the next year.

Bobby graduated from high school in 2000. Although he graduated two years later than scheduled, he walked onto the stage with only a cane for support and accepted his diploma. He has no sign of brain damage. Nikken magnets help restore his body to the best working order.

"I am still acquaintances with Bobby on Facebook," I told Dr. Todd.

She sat back in her chair in amazement. "Everything you are telling me, and all of your actions come from your heart. You are truly a generous person with a fighting spirit. You are proving to me that you do not have a problem fighting for other people. Now it is time for you to stand for yourself. Now is the time to put yourself first and concentrate only on the positives."

I couldn't believe how much confidence she was instilling in me. I thought my life was worthless and over after everything that had happened with Tony.

"I have an exercise for you," she continued. "Close your eyes and picture yourself on a beach. When you feel stress entering your body, picture the stress as the waves. Send the stress out with the waves. Breathe in positive thoughts and exhale negative thoughts."

I started to laugh. "If I am going to picture myself on a beach, I'm going to imagine myself being thin." Even our laughter eased some of my stress.

"Being on a beach reminds me of when I saved my husband from drowning."

"What? I can hardly wait to hear this story. I wish I could have a drink while working."

"This is definitely a vodka story. No good story ever started by eating a salad."

In January 1999, I was still part of the Nikken family. I welcomed the challenges of starting a new business and was honored to be part of their organization. I never made much money selling the products because I found myself giving most of it away to help people in pain.

About a month before Tony died, I arrived home after attending a Nikken event. He was already in bed. Only at that point did I suspect that he may be seeing someone else. I remember smelling the shirt that he placed in the basket to go to the cleaners. It smelled of perfume.

On January 31, 1999, Tony and I took a ten-day cruise with more than one hundred Nikken representatives and their families. I had never been on a cruise before and decided to book a suite. The cabin was a thousand square feet and had two balconies. The suite had a full-sized bathroom, a dressing room, a king-sized bed, and a large sectional sofa. Talk about luxury. I felt like a princess.

We entered the port of George Town in Grand Cayman with great excitement. I had never snorkeled before and was excited to try. I was an excellent swimmer (Delaware State Champion for five years in my teens), but Tony was not a very good swimmer at all.

I envisioned the depth of the water shallow with small fish. We signed up for an excursion with twenty other people. After a short safety session, we were all ready to dive into the water and explore, but Tony appeared hesitant to get into the water.

"Is anything wrong?" I asked. "No worries, I'll wait for you."

"That's okay," he told me. "I just need a little more time to get ready. Go and enjoy yourself. I'll be with you shortly."

I went with a group of ten people. We swam about half a football field length away from the boat. I was diving for almost an hour with no thought of anything except the turquoise blue water and the colorful fish dashing past us like they had to catch a bus.

I wondered where Tony was and began my search to find him. The boat was so far away that it appeared to be a rowboat from my distance. I started to swim toward the boat in search of Tony when I saw a man in distress. He was struggling for air as he waved his hands to get someone's attention.

I was about ten feet away from the man when he disappeared beneath the surface of the water. I dove down and grabbed the man's life jacket, pulling him back up to the surface.

"Sir, you are okay. No need to worry. You're safe now," I told the man. Then I looked at his face. I had just saved Tony.

Now as I sat in Dr. Todd's office, I shook my head at the memory. "Tony would tell the story just as it happened. But he'd end his story by saying, 'Do you know the worst part about Janet saving my life? Having her remind me of it every day.'"

Dr. Todd looked pensive. "Let's think about your story for a minute. Your husband killing himself after you saved him from drowning is almost like an oxymoron. I feel that one of the reasons your husband died by suicide was that he considered his life to be unworthy and unimportant. In reality, you valued your husband's life more than he valued it."

That was the first time I'd thought about it that way. "Tony lived his life intentionally hurting other people to feel better about himself," I admitted. "What goes around, comes around. Whether it's good or whether it's bad, it comes back to you."

Dr. Todd looked at her watch. We were past our hour-long appointment. "Listen," she said. "I don't have another patient today. Would you mind staying a little longer? I don't want to wait until our next session to hear your last story."

I laughed. "I have nowhere to go but home. Though I'm glad you have the time. I saved the best story for last. This story taught me not to underestimate the power of prayer or the power of blessed oils. I discovered firsthand that when God steps in, miracles happen."

One time when Tony was out of the country on business, I headed to Immaculate Heart of Mary Church in Wilmington for mass. I was running late and arrived just a few minutes before the church bells rang. My favorite pew was not available, so I sat a few rows behind.

When I knelt to pray before mass began, I noticed an older woman sitting in a front pew across the aisle. She appeared very frail and wore large sunglasses. Parked in front of the pew was a folded wheelchair. *She must be blind*, I thought.

More than 750 parishioners filled the church. The service started as usual. Monsignor Lemon gave his opening prayers, fellow parishioners read Bible passages, and we all sang the opening hymns. Father Bob began his sermon. He spoke for about five minutes when I noticed the older woman collapsed in the pew. Her husband, also frail, grabbed his cane to support himself and then attempted to assist her.

"Father Bob, stop!" I yelled out.

He lifted his head for a moment, then continued to read. I ran into the aisle, waving my hands in the air, and rushed to the woman. "Stop your sermon! We need a doctor! Is there a doctor in the house? I think this woman had a heart attack!"

Two men ran down the aisle to help. One said we needed to lift her off the pew and lay her on the floor. I attempted to support and soon realized that I was not strong enough and quickly moved out of the way.

Once on the floor, her husband checked for a pulse, and he could not find one. He began to perform CPR. His quick response made me think that he had executed the same task before.

A woman who greets parishioners as they enter the church walked steadfastly down the aisle to see what the commotion was.

I stood up. "Call 911, now!" I turned my attention back to the woman lying on the floor and overheard her husband pleading with her. "Carmen, please stay with me." He continued to perform CPR with persistent determination.

The woman started breathing on her own, and we all sighed with relief. But after fifteen minutes, there was still no sign of the paramedics. Suddenly, Carmen began gasping for air. I checked her pulse, and it was almost nonexistent.

Two women ran down the aisle with a defibrillator in tow. They attached the pads to Carmen's body. The silence continued to fill the room. The only sound was the defibrillator's recorded instructions on how to operate the equipment.

The final instruction was to remove the backing and place the blue pads directly on the person's chest. The voice said, "Stay clear and do not touch the person, then press the AED's Analyze button." The machine checked the person's heart rhythm. If a shock was needed, the AED would let us know when to deliver it.

Out of fear, Carmen's husband cried out, "Stop! I think she's breathing on her own." But she wasn't, so we got to work with the defibrillator again.

I hope this works, or she's going to die. Where are *the paramedics?*

After three shocks to restart her heart, Carmen's heart started beating on its own and her breathing normalized. She lay on the floor with her husband by her side.

Monsignor Lemon calmly walked down the aisle carrying a small paper cup. I never thought of his mission other than thinking that he would provide Carmen with a drink of water for dehydration. My split-second thought was wrong. He leaned down and anointed her forehead with blessed oil, making a sign of the cross. "Through this holy anointing may the Lord in His love and mercy help you with the grace of the Holy Spirit. May the Lord who frees you from sin save you and raise you." Then he started to say the Lord's Prayer.

"Our Father who art in heaven, hallowed be Thy name. Thy kingdom come; Thy will be done on earth as it is in heaven. Give us this day our daily bread; and forgive us our trespasses as we forgive those who trespass against us. And lead us not into temptation but deliver us from evil. Amen."

As he prayed, I looked around the church and found 750 parishioners on their knees, saying the prayer in unison.

The Monsignor started to make the sign of the cross on Carmen's forehead, but she reached up and grabbed his hand.

"Monsignor Lemon, am I going to die?"

"I do not know, my dear," he said. "You are absolved from all your sins. May God be with you."

My heart fell into my stomach when Carmen's heart stopped again. The two ladies who had been working on her reactivated the defibrillator with great urgency. Once again, they followed the instructions. Success! Once again, her heart started, and she was breathing on her own.

Thirty minutes passed, and there was still no sign of the paramedics. Parishioners continued to kneel and started chanting the rosary prayer aloud. Silence was replaced with the entire congregation reciting the Hail Mary Prayer.

"Hail Mary, full of grace. Our Lord is with thee. Blessed are thou among women, and blessed is the fruit of thy womb, Jesus. Holy Mary, Mother of God, pray for us sinners now and at the hour of our death. Amen."

It was the most empowering act of faith I had ever witnessed. They continued the prayer incessantly.

I found myself lost in the memory until Dr. Todd spoke up. "I understand why this is your favorite story. You are truly a woman of faith. I can feel your experience and feel your heart as you tell it. But where were the paramedics? Do you know why it took them so long to arrive?"

I shook my head. "I don't know. My best guess is that God was performing a miracle in front of 750 people and needed a little more time to complete it."

About ten minutes after Monsignor Lemon walked back up the aisle, a police officer arrived and confirmed the need for emergency assistance. Ten minutes later, two paramedics arrived with a gurney. They swept Carmen away as quickly as possible. The look on their faces was memorable. It appeared that they never witnessed a divine intervention before. That was my first time, too.

Monsignor Lemon followed the ambulance and stayed by Carmen's side. The following day I called him to see how Carmen was doing.

"When the emergency room doctors examined Carmen and tested her heart, there were no signs that she had a heart attack, so they sent her home to rest."

"That's crazy! We all witnessed her heart stop at least three times." Then it hit me. "I think we witnessed one of God's miracles right in front of our very eyes."

"Yes, we did, my dear," the Monsignor replied. "Yes, we did!"

Several months later, Carmen returned to the church. In the parking lot, after mass, I introduced myself. She started to cry and thanked me for saving her life. She said that she felt peace during the traumatic event because of my soft voice and by looking into my green eyes.

I laughed at the craziness of it all! My eyes used to be blue. When I gave birth to my daughter, my eye color changed to a vibrant green, and my daughter's eyes are blue.

Carmen and I talked a few times after that event. Her faith continued to grow, and she was grateful for God's intervention and her second chance at life.

Dr. Todd sat back in her chair, tears filling her eyes. I was crying too. "I can honestly say that I have listened to many stories over the years. Yours is the first that has moved me to tears." She dabbed at her eyes. "Your stories are amazing. Your husband did not deserve someone like you. Your heart is pure, and I can see you have had a fulfilling life helping others. Each day remind yourself of these stories and the gift of life that you gave to others, with God's helping hands. God often performs miracles through everyday people."

Her words encouraged me.

"Did you ever take the opportunity to read more about the power of blessed oils?" she asked.

"Yes! I was not aware of their powers until I read about them. I found that blessed oils do not have magical healing powers in and of themselves. The oils symbolize God's grace and heal believers through their faith. It is a sacrament similar to holy water, designed to help people grow in their spiritual lives. And they help increase people's devotion to their faith."

At that moment, I knew in my heart that my real healing power would come only from God. My love-hate relationship with Him was now leaning more toward love, and I found peace.

I told myself not to worry if I did not always feel His presence. I knew in my heart that He is never blind to our tears, never deaf to our prayers, and never silent to our pain. I knew that God sees and hears everything, and when the day comes, in God's timing, He will reward me for getting through my pain and helping others.

I left Dr. Todd's office feeling empowered. *I'm learning more about myself with each conversation.* And I was ridding myself of my low self-esteem.

Following her advice, I learned to take deeper breaths and close my eyes to picture myself on a beach when stressed. I learned how to calm a racing heart, and I realized that healing does not come overnight; it's a process.

I couldn't change the outcome of what Tony had done—both in his life and through his death, but I could control how I responded to it. *Today is the first day of the rest of my life,* I realized for the first time since Tony's death. *And I know things are going to be okay.*

Acknowledging the good that you already have in your life
is the foundation for all abundance.
—Eckhart Tolle

CHAPTER 6

TRYING TO MOVE FORWARD

The worst kind of hurt is betrayal because it means
someone was willing to hurt you to make themselves feel better.
—Author Unknown

A week after my psychologist's appointment, I received a phone call from my friend Larry. He invited me to go to dinner with him and his wife, Ruth. They were friends with Tony and his ex-wife, and they became my friends too. Larry owned a fast-food pizza and sandwich shop.

The first time I met Larry, he told me about a six-foot snowstorm where he closed his shop and sent his employees home, because he'd been concerned for their safety.

As he was closing up, he remembered an elderly disabled man who depended on daily deliveries to eat. He returned to his shop, made a steak sandwich, and personally delivered it. When he arrived at the man's house, he was upset by what he saw.

"Why were you so upset?" I asked.

"I felt sorry for the man," Larry said. "He's been bedridden for years. The only people he sees are his daughters occasionally, his nurses, and his sandwich delivery man."

This scenario seems very familiar to me, I thought and then asked, "What is the man's name?"

"Robert Benson," Larry said.

"The handicapped man who you met is my father," I told him. "My father has multiple sclerosis. He was diagnosed in his thirties and has been bedridden for the past three years. He and my mother have been divorced for more than fifteen years. My sisters and I have tried many times to get him out of the house so he can be properly cared for. However, he is too stubborn and will not leave his home."

What a small world, I thought.

Larry, Ruth, Tony, and I would go out to dinner at least once a month. Additionally, Tony and Larry met for lunch several times a month. They had been friends for more than twenty-five years.

Now at dinner, Larry told me that he knew about many of Tony's affairs when Tony was with his ex-wife and then with me.

About a year before Tony died, Ruth asked Larry if Tony was having an affair, and Larry told her yes. At that, she refused to have dinner with Tony because she was a great friend of mine.

"Why didn't you tell me?" I asked, feeling stunned.

"I knew that if you found out that Tony was having an affair, you would divorce him. Walking away was easier than getting involved. I'm sorry."

"I never knew that," I admitted. "Tony would just tell me that Ruth was very loud and he did not want to be around her." I felt disgusted. "He was always making excuses to shed a better light on himself." *Once again, that was another lie.*

"I had lunch with Tony two months before he died," Larry said. "His phone rang, and an outraged woman was screaming on the other end. He told me that he just ended a two-year relationship with a woman. She was an alcoholic and threatened to tell you about their affair. Tony assured her that you already knew."

My jaw dropped. "I didn't know anything!" Then I thought about a phone number from an Italian deli I'd found on a piece of paper in Tony's sock drawer. I'd done some research and discovered that the woman's name was Kathy, and she lived a few blocks from me. She also had a reputation for being a very loose woman. *This woman's name was not on the list that my daughter and son-in-law shared with me.* I wondered how many more women would surface.

"Listen, Janet, there's more. I have no proof of this, but—" he paused, looking uncomfortable. "I overheard a lot of Tony's phone conversations. I believe Tony was involved with something illegal and possibly the Philadelphia mafia."

I didn't want to believe it could be true, but my mind began to recall memories. Lots of things hadn't made sense at the time, but now . . . *Had Tony been selling stolen automotive parts and possibly laundering money?* I wondered.

Although Tony kept his business life secretive, he told me that his company paid to have a cottage built in Australia next to a client's house and had a custom sign made naming the cottage "Holleywood." He said that they also paid for a new roof and driveway on another client's home. When I asked Tony why his company did these "acts of kindness," he said, "They are very loyal clients. It is our way of thanking them for their business."

Tony started selling used golf carts in addition to automotive parts to his customer in Australia. On several occasions I asked Tony why he got involved in a new business of selling used golf carts. He said that he found out there was a shortage and felt he would capitalize on the opportunity. I cannot begin to imagine what he had shipped in the golf carts.

He had business dealings with people who lived in California, Texas, and Florida, as well as offshore business.

Another person of interest was Eduardo, who lived in Venezuela. Tony and Eduardo were friends and business partners for more than twenty years. One day their business and friendship ended abruptly. Eduardo attended the dinners in Philadelphia with Tony when he was in town.

One time, Eduardo was visiting for business. While in the States, his attorney contacted him about a criminal offense charge against him in Venezuela.

When Tony told me about it, he claimed there was a misunderstanding about a shopping center that Eduardo owned. He lived with us for three months while a team of attorneys attempted to straighten out the mess so he could reenter his country.

Police arrested Eduardo at the Simon Bolivar International Airport when he arrived back in his home country. He spent one year in a "gentleman's prison." It was more like a country club atmosphere for the "untouchables." Tony never heard from him again. Several months before Tony's death, he saw Eduardo at an automotive convention in Las Vegas. According to Tony, they never spoke, and when they saw each other, each walked the other way.

As I listened to Larry sharing his suspicions and me collaborating with what little I knew, I couldn't help but be grateful that my appointment with Dr. Todd was only a few days away.

I'd had such a great appointment with her during our previous time together in which her comments gave me the courage to start believing in myself and working on raising my self-esteem. But now when I arrived at her office, I felt distraught.

Dr. Todd picked up on it right away. "Are you okay? After our last appointment, I felt certain that today's visit would be an extension of the jubilant way you felt when you left."

"I was perfect—until I had dinner with a friend of Tony's and his wife." I replayed our conversation. "Dinner was going great until he felt the need to tell me about Tony's affairs and his alleged connection to the Philadelphia mafia."

"I am sorry that people are coming out of the woodworks and feel the need to clear their minds of the secret information they held about your husband. I can guarantee they are doing it more for themselves than for you. At some point, you are going to have to decide to say *no more*! You need to move forward with your life and not backward. To move forward, you must put the past behind you. It was your husband's choice to die. Now you must make your choice to live. Your goal must be to settle Tony's estate as soon as possible."

"I agree with you 100 percent." I committed to call my attorney the following day to see if there was a way to expedite closing the estate. For the rest of my appointment, we concentrated only on the positives and steps I could take in my life to move forward.

The next day I called my attorney and found out that he spoke with Tony's family attorney the day before and found that we were miles apart from a settlement with no ending in sight.

The only leverage I had was the control of my husband's headstone for his gravesite. Through my attorney, I let the other side know that I would only approve the headstone placement when the estate settled.

I did not like myself for taking action. I had no other recourse to recover money that was lawfully mine. Every day that I delayed the headstone placement, it destroyed my husband's family, primarily his parents and daughters, and crushed a bit of myself. This was not what I wanted, but I felt I had no other recourse.

I felt as if I was destroying myself from the inside out. Anger filled every heartbeat and every step I took. I had no idea where I was going to find the strength to endure.

My father-in-law died six months after my husband. I am sure he died from a broken heart. I did not attend the funeral. Even though my father-in-law treated me nicely, I didn't feel comfortable putting myself into a position in which I needed to interact with other members of the family.

Tony's daughters made a marker for their father's grave out of paper and covered it with plastic. Months later, they made a marker stamped in metal. It was a joyous occasion and a sigh of relief for his family and me when I finally approved putting a headstone on his grave more than a year later.

One year after my husband's death—Friday, December 13, 2002—brought intense emotional pain. I managed to emotionally get through birthdays, our wedding anniversary, and select dates that we celebrated, but I knew this upcoming anniversary date would be the most difficult.

As the date quickly approached, the thought of getting through another Christmas season and mentally preparing myself for the first anniversary of Tony's death was something that made me sick to my stomach.

I decided to have a Christmas party at my home on December 14. Although I was hesitant and not in a festive mood, I felt it would be best to surround myself with family and friends. I needed to engage my mind with something useful instead of something terrible.

Once I made the decision and sent out invitations, I experienced the ramifications of negative thinking. Some of the people who were closer to Tony declined because they felt I was celebrating Tony's death. They were friends I had not seen in almost a year. They did not understand.

My sister Peggy owned a catering company called "The Upper Crust" in Wilmington. She took over the entire process of decorating my home in addition to catering the food. Her decorating skills are worthy of a magazine cover, and her cooking skills would challenge any master chef.

The night before the party, the anniversary of Tony's death, I took two Ambien to sleep. I also drank a vodka gimlet to calm my nerves.

Am I making the right decision to have a party? I wondered, fearing that I was taking that step a little too soon.

I went to bed and took my usual position of lying on my stomach to go to sleep. As I drifted off to sleep—exhausted physically, mentally, and emotionally—I felt a weight on my body. I had experienced the heaviness before, but my body's pressure this night was more substantial than usual. The weight was so heavy that I could not pull my arms out from under my body. I felt trapped.

As I struggled to pull my arms out from underneath my body, my head turned toward Tony's side of the bed. There he lay next to me, blood pouring out of his eyes, nose, and mouth. Had my actions angered him? I concluded that Tony was not happy with me having a party and decided to express his displeasure in a way that I would never forget.

I woke up screaming and could not get the image out of my head. I visualized myself sitting in a pool of blood on top of my saturated mattress.

I turned on the lights, and looked at the clock. It was 2:00 a.m. I walked into the living room and sat on the sofa motionless for hours. In the morning, I called my daughter and sisters and told them of my horrifying dream. I had many anxiety attacks throughout the day. I felt as though I was losing a part of myself.

I looked around my home, filled with the blessings of Christmas and the magnificent holiday decorations. I could not imagine greeting and socializing with more than fifty guests within a few hours.

The servers, Mark and Summer, arrived three hours before the scheduled event. When Mark walked in, he gasped with horror at the first sight of me. I knew I must have looked very disheveled. "What happened to you?"

I certainly was not going to share the details of my dream with anyone other than my immediate family. But I had to tell him something. "I had a horrible dream about my husband last night," I confessed. "I would like to cancel the party, but I know it's too late."

"We are here now," he said. "Go and get ready for your guests. Let me fix you a strong drink."

"That's why they make vodka." I said, trying my best to lighten the mood.

"Relax in a tub of hot water and light some candles."

It sounded like an excellent idea.

I lit more than a dozen candles, turned off all the lights, and sat motionless in the bathtub with hot water. I was unsure how I would muster the courage to meet and greet and pretend that I was having a good time at my party.

Tony is very angry with me, I thought as I soaked among the suds. *What a horrible way to show his displeasure. I am a basket case. How am I going to pull myself together and pretend that everything is wonderful?*

Peggy arrived right before my guests and fixed me another vodka gimlet. "Shake a leg, Juanita," she said as she handed it to me.

When my guests arrived, I was still soaking in the tub. Emotionally, I prepared myself to stay in the bathtub until the next day. Mentally, I talked myself into getting ready for my party.

When I finally greeted my guests, I was not feeling any pain. The alcohol, hot bath, and anxiety medication relaxed my nerves. Christmas music filled the air, and guests dressed in their best holiday outfits, added to the evening's ambiance. A bartender prepared drinks while other servers walked around my home serving hors d'oeuvres. It would have been a perfect evening if I did not have the constant vision of Tony's bloody face from the night before.

The last guest left around midnight. My sisters, daughter, and her husband left a little later. Now I was alone again and terrified of going to bed. I was afraid to go to sleep, yet I was too exhausted not to. Even knowing that taking Ambien can have side effects, I knew I would not be able to sleep without aid.

The next day I woke up filled with anger. I felt as though I was on the verge of destroying myself. My anger intensified with every step and every breath I took. Once again, I questioned the existence of a God who would allow me to go through so much pain.

I questioned why I would or could not let go of the anger. But deep down I knew. I felt that if I forgave my husband, it would be like saying I dismissed the actions of his betrayals and his death.

No way was I going to agree to that. So, without being consciously aware of my actions, I began the process of destroying myself a little bit each day. My life was a disaster. My healing process was on a physical and emotional rollercoaster, and I was uncertain how I would survive.

Because I had depended heavily on Ambien, I thought it best to learn more about it. I discovered that Ambien is also called a hypnotic. It affects the brain's chemicals that may cause unbalanced and sleep problems, impair a person's thinking or reactions, and cause difficult breathing. Some people using this medicine have engaged in driving, eating, walking, making phone calls, having sex, and later having no memory of the activity. But it was the final warning that stopped me cold: "Do not take Ambien if you have consumed alcohol."

I thought the best thing that I should do was concentrate on the positive to let go of the negative. I increased writing in my "Positive Quotes Journal" and prayed that my actions would help me heal sooner than later.

I found a quote by Lewis K. Bendele that inspired me to write down my goals and take action: "A man without a plan for his day is lost before he starts." I needed a plan.

A few days later, I decided to go to the movies. It was the first day I dared to do something on my own. I had always enjoyed going to the movies by myself and sometimes with Tony. This day I felt confident to be on my own.

I selected *It's a Beautiful Mind* starring Russell Crowe, Jennifer Connelly, and Ed Harris—three of my favorite actors. After I purchased my ticket, I stopped off at the popcorn counter. But when I walked into the theater, I found every seat occupied. I was not surprised since it was a Sunday and the middle of winter. People needed to get out of the house and still stay warm.

The only other movie with the same schedule was *Hart's War* with Bruce Willis. Before Bruce became a famous actor, he lived in Carneys Point, New Jersey. His father was in the military. His mother, Marlene Willis, lived in Delaware and worked for The Bank of Delaware. I had the opportunity to meet Marlene on several occasions and felt that I knew Bruce, even though I had never met him. The movie seemed like a safe choice.

The theater was also crowded. The only seat available was in the eighth row, a little too close for my liking. It made me feel as if I were in the movie. *Hart's War* is an American thriller drama about a World War II prisoner of war (POW) camp based on the novel by John Katzenbach.

I was captivated by the movie until the final scene. (Spoiler alert.) It had a shocking ending. After escaping from the POW camp, Colonel William McNamara (Bruce Willis) voluntarily returned to the base to accept responsibility in order to save his commander for helping soldiers escape. The scene ended with McNamara being shot in the head and falling to the ground.

My husband's weapon of choice was a gun. The first time I saw my husband after his death was at his viewing. Although the funeral director reversed the normal position of Tony's body lying in the casket to present his better side, I occasionally wondered about the appearance of the other side of his head. I did not have to wonder any longer.

That last scene sent me into a state of shock. My body went numb. My legs were so weak that I could not stand. I remained in the theater while people cleaned the popcorn off the floor, and soon the lights went dim. I sat unable to move for a very long time.

When I finally mustered the strength to leave, I walked in a trance to my car. Once inside, I found myself screaming and crying out of control.

I bruised my hands and thought I had fractured a finger because of banging my fists and hands against the steering wheel and windows. My anxiety attacks were getting worse by the minute.

"Help me, God, please help me!" I yelled. I felt as though I was having an out of body experience.

I called my daughter and sisters for help, but no one answered their phones. I knew I was incapable of driving. My emotions had gotten the best of me.

I lay in a fetal position in my freezing car for longer than I can remember. Finally I made another call to my sister Billie.

"Hello?" she said.

"Thank you, God!" I said through tears. "Billie, please help me. I need help now."

"Where are you?" her sweet voice had immediately turned to fear. "What happened? Were you in a car accident?"

"No. I am in the parking lot of the movie theater on Naaman's Road. I saw the movie *Hart's War.* In the last scene, an enemy soldier shot Bruce Willis in his head."

She gasped, clearly understanding my plight. "Stay right where you are. I'll be there in a few minutes." True to her promise, she arrived within ten minutes.

When she opened the car door, she immediately gathered me into her arms and held me for a long time until I stopped crying and was able to regain my composure. "I'm here now. You are safe. I love you," she said repeatedly.

She took me to her son and daughter-in-law's house in Chadds Ford, Pennsylvania, where we had dinner. Then I spent the night at Billie's home, took two anxiety pills, and went to bed. I was too much of a basket case to be on my own.

As much as I wanted to start my healing process again, I had too many unanswered questions. Other people's comments and opinions continued to make me angry. Still, I felt that to have peace, I needed to settle scores with the women with whom I suspected Tony was having affairs. This part of my life was indeed a roller coaster. As much as I wanted to put the past behind me, emotionally, I could not.

A few days later, two close friends, Margie and Sandy, accompanied me to Sullivan's Restaurant to accuse a waitress named Lynne for having an affair with my husband. One time Tony and I had dinner at Sullivan's. Tony requested Lynne as our waitress. He greeted her with a warm hello and a kiss on her lips, then he pressed his body against hers. I became angry and commented, "What are you doing? Why are you greeting Lynne that way?" He'd replied, "I don't know why you're angry. She is your friend too." I never returned to the restaurant with Tony again.

Now when I entered, Lynne ran up to me, crying. She asked the hostess for my friends and me to sit at her station.

I told Lynne that Tony had many affairs during our marriage and said that the sad part was that I thought she was one of them.

Lynne's face registered shock and she began to cry again. "I would never do that. I have too much respect for you!"

"Did Tony ever approach you about it?"

"No," she tried to reassure me.

During dinner we discussed how many affairs Tony had engaged in and how I had been in the dark about them all. Then Sandy put down her fork and stared seriously at me. "A friend of mine had a dream about you. She saw that your life is in danger."

"Has your friend ever had a similar dream about anyone else?"

"Yes."

"What happened?"

She shifted uncomfortably in her seat and replied that something had happened to them but she would not give me the details. "I'm not trying to freak you out, but I do fear for your safety."

But it did freak me out. On the way home I called my daughter and told her about my evening. She was upset with my friends. She knew that I was still recovering from the anxiety attacks of a few days before.

My "friends'" actions and comments steered me into having a nervous breakdown. I increased my anxiety medication and didn't leave my home for months. I only felt safe when members of my family escorted me any place. I walked away from my friends of twenty-five years.

I spent much of my time reading and watching television. Although I wrote daily in a journal, I created a third journal for more quotations, positive affirmations, and Bible passages. I continued my ritual: if I felt hopeless, I sought out Bible passages on hope. When I felt anger, I explored Bible passages on anger.

My mission was to heal; however, the healing process was becoming increasingly difficult. I realized that the process was going to take a lot more time than I expected. From where I was sitting, it looked like it was going to take a lifetime.

I was intrigued by a quote from Lord Chesterfield: "I recommend you take care of the minutes, for the hours will take care of themselves." And I reminded myself about the card that my sister Diane sent to me and the message she wrote inside it: "Take baby steps, just like Mackenzie." My granddaughter, Mackenzie, was nine months old and was just beginning to walk.

I decided to put the final chapter of asking questions about other women behind me, just one more time. One of the messages that Tony said to me after his death was through the medium named Patricia: "I am not hurting you. You are hurting yourself." But what Tony did not understand was that I felt like his pain was my pain, and my pain was his pain. It's only natural for married people to share in each other's joy, pain, and sorrow.

When we lay in bed next to each other, I would wrap my body around his body. It felt like we were one person. Internally, I thought that I was experiencing my pain and experiencing the pain and disappointment that Tony encountered before his death.

I knew that my most significant challenge was to put the past behind me to move forward.

I could not imagine how someone would think that suicide was the only answer to a problem. I wondered why Tony would not ask for help or tell the truth and plead for mercy and understanding with a promise to love me and be loyal to me.

Reliving my husband's death and the circumstances around it constantly reopened my wounded heart. I often wondered if the pain would ever go away. But I knew I had to choose to remember the good times more than the bad. One thing I knew for sure: Tony did not kill himself because of another woman.

But slowly I began to understand a piece of God's puzzle for my life that previously did not make sense. I realized that God sometimes chooses individuals to start the process of creating more to help others. The essential point is that it took my husband to die tragically, with a wayward life, for me to discover my true life's purpose.

Slowly as I worked through the healing process, getting my fear and anxiety under control, I began to see that Tony's death could bring something good from it. God showed me that I am part of His bigger plan to help others get through their pain. I am a more credible witness. People tend to listen to a credible witness who has survived, knowing that we share a similar pain.

I remember people coming up to me after my husband's death and saying: "I know how you feel."

I became outraged and declared, "You have no idea how I feel, and I pray to God that you never do." That shut them up very quickly.

When I decided to write to God in a journal to release my pain, I thought my words were falling onto deaf ears. My life seemed to be moving two steps behind for every step that I took forward. Looking back, I recognized that God frequently spoke to me with His silent words. I was the one with the selective hearing.

After reading many quotes, I decided to create a quote based on my inner feelings. I believe this quote with my whole heart.

There is no way that God would make me go through so much pain without having something wonderful on the other side.
—Janet V. Grillo

CHAPTER 7

MESSAGES FROM THE OTHER SIDE

Life can only be understood backwards, but it must be lived forwards.
—Soren Kierkegaard

When I was six years old, I drowned. I remember playing a game in a pool with other children. A parent suggested that we play a game where we all held onto each other's feet. The chain of children extended to five. An adult was the engine of the train, and I was the caboose.

The last thing I remembered was being at the bottom of the deep end of the pool, trying to get any swimmer's attention, waving my hands as they swam overhead. My efforts were not successful, and I drowned. I do not remember the rescue attempt, nor do I remember being resuscitated.

I do remember my spirit leaving my body and overlooking many people who were crying while some worked to bring me back to life. I saw a bright light, but I never saw friends and family encouraging me to walk with them to the other side. I merely saw my lifeless body lying on the ground. I never spoke about my out-of-body experience to anyone. As a six-year-old, I thought the experience normal. I did, however, think about it often—especially that so many people cried and worried about me when it had happened.

That brought me a lot of comfort. Being a middle child, I often felt ignored or neglected. I always felt different. Any time I spoke about my big dreams, my family would always put down, saying I was too big of a dreamer. At least someone cared, I thought whenever I remembered my experience, seeing everybody surrounding me.

When I was twenty-one, I visited a bookstore. As I browsed, I came upon *Life After Life* by Raymond Moody, a study of one hundred people who experienced a clinical death and were revived. They tell, in their own words, what lies beyond death. In 1991, he claims to have had his own near-death experience when he attempted suicide. He says that an undiagnosed thyroid condition affected his mental state, causing him to try to take his life. Today he is known as the father of the modern NDE (near-death experience) movement, and his work transformed the world, revolutionizing the way we think about death and what lies beyond.

For the first time, thanks to this book, I felt more confident to talk about my experience without fear that everyone would think I was crazy.

Ever since my near-death experience, I've felt that I have a close connection to people who have died. Many times, I feel the presence of others, and sometimes I have conversations with them. It's as if I talk to them in a different dimension.

The best way to understand this connection is to imagine talking to someone in another room. Because of my sixth sense, I have always been fascinated with psychics and mediums. Occasionally, I would visit for the entertainment. Sometimes, I found hope in a psychic reading.

In 1985 I met with a psychic named Valerie. She was an older Italian woman with much wisdom. Valerie gave me comfort when she said that my life was going to change. She told me to expect a better job offer with a significant pay increase. She also told me that Tony and I would be purchasing a new home with many windows overlooking a river.

At the time, I did not have the vision, so I held onto what I would call a healthy skepticism. But both of Valerie's predictions came true.

I read stories about other suicide survivors who enlisted psychics' assistance after their loved one died by suicide. They said that though they would never get over their loss, they had a better understanding of their loved one's challenges that lead them to take their own lives.

Now with Tony's death placing a shadow over my life and our relationship, I reached out to several psychic mediums for guidance.

I lived a picture-perfect life with Tony, even though I found out that he'd had numerous affairs during our marriage. I knew that he had loved me and knew he was dead, but I still did not know why. I became relentless in my search for answers, feeling like a detective working a cold case.

A friend told me about Patricia, a medium who lived about ten miles from my house. "You should consult with her," my friend encouraged me.

I called Patricia and told her that my husband died by suicide, and I did not know why. She suggested that we meet at my home and declared that spirits channel best in familiar settings. I agreed, and we agreed to meet on February 5, 2003. I was pleased that she scheduled our meeting for two days after we spoke. My husband had been dead for fourteen months. Since many investigations ended without clarity, I looked forward to possibly receiving messages from the other side.

Patricia arrived at my home at 2:30 p.m. When I opened the door to greet her, I was pleasantly surprised. She was beautiful. She stood about five-feet tall, had short blonde hair and a perfect complexion.

"Hello, Janet," she said. Her soft voice immediately brought me comfort. As soon as she walked through the door, she turned and looked at me. "I had the strangest feeling while driving to your house. The atmosphere was angry, and the closer I came, I felt the anger's intensity strengthen. I have never experienced a feeling like that."

I wasn't sure what that meant, if anything, or how to respond.

We sat comfortably on the living room sofa. Rays of sunshine poured through the windows. Patricia closed her eyes to connect with Tony's spirit, while I sat patiently *and* impatiently with pen in hand and a notebook.

"Tony is very angry with you for making people feel uncomfortable with your questions," She said. "Your husband has many questions for you."

Though Patricia was still speaking, her statements appeared to come directly from Tony. "Why are you not concerned about my death? You appear to be more consumed with my affairs. I am not hurting you. You are hurting yourself. Leave it alone. My death had nothing to do with love. I married you and I was always there for you. You had everything. Don't let my affairs bother you. How can you take it so seriously? It was just a game. Some people drive fast cars, other people gamble. Sex with other women was my gambling."

Patricia stopped speaking, and I sat wondering how to take it all in.

Soon Patricia spoke again. "I got involved with some people I should not have gotten involved. They play for keeps."

I gasped, as chills went through my body. *Did Tony die by suicide or . . . is he saying he was murdered?* "Is my life in danger?" I asked quietly, tensing at what the response might be.

"Only if you keep pressing the issues."

"Who is Jimmy?" Patricia seemed to be asking on her own now. "The person your husband is referring to someone you would not suspect. Tony met a man in Las Vegas. He was involved too. The man has broad shoulders and dyed blonde hair. His natural hair is gray."

I felt scared, but couldn't think of anyone by that description. At that point, I suspected everybody Tony had had a relationship with—both personally and in business.

Then a name came to mind. "Do you mean John?" I asked. Six months before Tony's death, he drove to Pittsburgh with a man named

John and then continued to Cleveland to meet with clients. I never understood why John took the trip with him. John was not part of the automotive community.

Previously when I'd questioned Tony about his traveling companion, he said that he mentioned to John about his road trip, and John asked if he could tag along. Perhaps this was the man Tony was referring to about not suspecting.

But then I remembered that one of Tony's friends from Cleveland had an Italian father who lived in Canada and owned many Italian restaurants. Even though his client was successful, each year his father gave him hundreds of thousands of dollars in cash. He had a twenty-five-thousand-square-foot empty warehouse and lived in a ten-thousand-square-foot home. *Could he be the person?* "Tony's grief and loss were not present in that moment," Patricia said, breaking into my thoughts. "Your husband did not know how to love and share importance."

Again, her comment surprised me and I did not know what she meant. Tony liked the ambiance of the love provided by his family, home, and other people—and apparently other women. He loved himself more than anyone else.

I now believed that Tony was incapable of returning true love. I believed that he loved me and cared for me in his own way, even though he was not devoted to me.

"Your husband just doesn't get it," she said. "He has no signs of remorse. There are those who know why he killed himself."

"I think it's best that you stop asking about the circumstances around Tony's death," Patricia said. "I have a feeling that Tony cheated on someone, and they found out. I get the impression that Tony slept with the wrong person and later found out she was the wife of someone he knew."

Did Tony do something to someone who had the power to come after him?

I felt overwhelmed by the information she'd offered. Some of the mysterious pieces of the puzzle appeared to be taking form.

"Tony liked living on the edge," Patricia said. "It gave his life color." Then she switched into talking for Tony again. "I realized that I could not lie about my actions. There was no way I could get past this one."

I spoke directly to Tony. "Who did you spend the weekend with, right before your death?"

Tony told me that he flew to Chicago to meet with clients. But according to his credit card statement, he spent the weekend in Philadelphia. One night he stayed at the Adams Mark Hotel and one night at The Four Seasons. Apparently, he entertained two different women.

Tony did not mention any names.

"Were you with Laura and Judy?" I asked, running through a mental list of women.

"Yes."

Patricia chimed in on our conversation. "There is no emotion in your husband's voice when he talks about other women. I truly believe his actions were just a game."

Tony had a few last comments before the conversation ended. "Take a hard look at my friends. What do they get for it? Many people knew about each other. I am advising you. Don't do it for me. When people come to you with information, ask them why they are telling you. Ask them if they feel good about hurting you. Janet, get on with your life."

After Patricia left, I continued to ponder the experience. I wish I could have gotten on with my life. Anger was destroying me. And what kind of dangerous things had he been involved in? And . . . was I in danger?

And then I thought of Tony and his interactions with other women. How many women had he been with? Just the thought made me sick to my stomach.

I reflected back to the week Tony died, when Kristina—Tony's girlfriend #10, 11, 12, or one-night stand—and her husband were on vacation. They returned several days after the funeral, unaware of what had happened. When Kristina found out, through tears she asked if I would like to meet her for lunch.

We agreed. "Let's meet at the Columbus Inn," I suggested, my suspicions raising yet again. I chose that particular restaurant because I knew Tony and Kristina had been there once together. Tony had mentioned that he'd gone to the Columbus Inn one night and saw Kristina there.

"She was sitting alone at the bar, so I invited her to join me for drinks and dinner," he'd told me.

At the time, I thought it strange, because Kristina was married. *Why is a married woman sitting at a bar by herself drinking?* It didn't help my suspicions that Kristina and Tony had always appeared chummier than a normal friend relationship.

I arrived at the restaurant before Kristina and sat patiently waiting for my "friend" to arrive. A thousand thoughts went through my mind as I sought the right words to say to her when I confronted her with my suspicions. My main objective for confronting Kristina in person, rather than over the phone, was to see her reaction.

Kristina arrived and hugged me in condolence. We ordered and made small talk. When the food arrived, I knew it was time to set the bait.

"I've recently found out that Tony was involved with at least five women at the time of his death. I often wonder if there were any women in Wilmington that he did *not* engage in sex. For all I know," I said in a half-kidding tone, "you could have been one of Tony's girlfriends."

She grew furious. "What are you talking about?" she said in a loud voice. "Are you accusing me of having an affair with your husband?"

Other diners turned and looked at us.

I had received my answer. She had just given away her guilt.

"I was just kidding," I said calmly.

After our lunch, we never spoke again.

The more I thought about Tony's betrayal with these women, the more consumed I felt about getting revenge on them. I wanted to expose them when they least expected it. But then I reminded myself that I had been one of "the other women" eighteen years earlier.

I guess he loved me in the only way he could. I knew it was time to close the chapter on the "other women" and move on. Before I did, though, I felt the need to speak to another medium.

I met Amy through friends two years before we connected for a reading. But one day I found her business card sitting on my desk without any explanation of how it got there. I was attracted to Amy because she had many talents. In addition to being a psychic, she was a spiritual intuitive and healing medium. Her specialties included grief and loss, past life trauma recovery, proving the survival of soul, and life path development. She had an amazing talent for channeling the spirits of people who had died.

Because the accuracy of Amy's readings were spot on, she was in high demand. I had to wait two months for my appointment.

I was excited when Amy scheduled the appointment. Seeing her in action in addition to listening to her, enhanced my connection. She started with a prayer asking God for assistance with her channeling. I found the gesture confusing because Catholics are taught to denounce psychics and fortunetelling.

If that's true, so why am I doing this? I accused myself. Even though I knew it was wrong, according to Catholic teaching, I needed more information to close my cold-case investigation. So I dove ahead.

As we began our conversation, Amy started to laugh and looked away.

"What's so funny?" I asked.

"Your husband, mother, and father just walked in and sat on the sofa next to each other."

I glanced at the sofa across the room and tried to imagine them sitting next to each other on it.

"They are chomping at the bits to talk to you. Oh my, your husband is very handsome and tall with dark curly hair. You may not believe this, but he is winking at me. He is flirting with me."

I sighed. "Yes, that is my husband. You described him perfectly."

Prior to our appointment, I never spoke to Amy about Tony, other than to tell her that he had died by suicide. So I was shocked by her opening comments. "It was not your husband's decision to die. Someone else decided for him. He heard that he upset someone significant who had the reputation of ending people's lives. Your husband did not die where he was found. Someone connected to the mafia moved his body.

What is she talking about? Was this a mafia hit? It sounds like someone was with him when he died. Had Tony been forced to take his own life? I remembered him saying through Patricia, "There was no way I could get past this one." He did not have the option to walk away.

"Your husband owned many guns," Amy continued.

Her revelation caught me off guard. "My husband told me that he hated guns. Why would he buy a gun and take a delivery on the day of his death? Why wouldn't he use one of the guns that he owned, rather than buy a new one?"

"The guns your husband owned can be connected to law enforcement," Amy said. "His illegal actions were associated with many levels of the government."

Then just as Patricia had done, Amy made a comment from Tony. "You can accuse me of many things, but you can never accuse me of being a rat."

This sounds crazy! But could this possibly be true? Who was this man I'd been married to for so many years? I had no clue. I was uncertain what to believe and what not to believe. I shook my head. *How can one person cause so much trauma and pain in so many lives? Did Tony ever love me? Or was that just part of his game?*

As if reading my thoughts, Amy said, "Tony wants me to tell you that he loved you very much and never wanted to hurt you. Your husband does not understand why you are still upset, even after he told you it was just a game. He says he was a gambler and bet on everything." Then she started to laugh.

"What are you laughing about?"

"Your husband is a funny guy. He said that the one thing he would never bet on was you thinking about writing a book about his life."

I joined in on the laughter. "He definitely would have lost that bet." (The funny thing is that God knew the plans for my life way before I did. I started writing in journals in 2002, and did not start to write this book until 2017.)

Though I appreciated what I heard from Amy, it left me with more confusion than before. And for the next several months, I continued to struggle with all the unanswered questions.

My sister Billie's husband died from a heart attack six months after Tony's death. One day she asked me to go with her to an intuitive spiritual counselor and psychic medium, I agreed. Billie had never entertained the services of a psychic and was curious to try.

When we entered Reverend Donna's office, about ninety minutes from Billie's house, we both felt immediate comfort. The waiting room had the appearance of a doctor's office with the exception that the room was dimly lit. Many spiritual magazines graced the tables, including an album filled with letters of gratitude.

Reverend Donna entered the room. She reminded me of my mother—small in stature with medium-length, red wavy hair. She introduced herself and asked which of us wanted to have our reading first.

"I will," Billie said.

They exited into a small room off the waiting room. I was hoping to hear their conversation, but the walls did not allow it.

After thirty minutes, the door opened. Billie gave me a thumbs up. Now it was my turn. Two white wicker chairs sat across from each other. We both sat, but the room was so small, our knees almost touched.

Donna closed her eyes and smiled as though someone were whispering into her ear. "The first person visiting you today is a woman with dark hair. She is not your mother. She appears to be your grandmother. The woman is referring to you as 'Little Janet.'"

My jaw dropped. None of my siblings knew that my mother's family called me Little Janet. My mother named me after her youngest sister, Janet.

"Your parents are standing beside you. Your mother says that they know you have many questions and are dealing with many issues and challenges. Do not worry. You are a strong woman, and everything will be more than just okay."

My mother's words, coming through Donna, gave me comfort. But I also knew that the statement could have been said to anyone sitting in my chair.

"Your husband is here," Donna continued. "He says, 'I love you very much and I am sorry for everything. I now have a clearer picture of the life I lived. I wish I had chosen to live without the affairs. You loved me with all your heart, and I took your love for granted.'" Then Donna smiled. "You are going to get a new set of golf clubs."

My jaw dropped again. I had just ordered a new set of clubs the day before!

Without warning, Donna opened her eyes very wide and stared at me. "Oh my!"

"What is it?"

"You have the same ability that I have. Do you ever talk to spirits?"

"I have conversations with them all the time, when I feel their presence."

"You have tangibly heard your husband's voice twice since he died."

I nodded. "You are right! It was both one of the scariest and most comforting feelings I've ever had."

"The best place to talk to spirits is close to water," Donna said. "The ocean is the best place. Spirits tend to gather near water."

Afterward, I went home and did a Google search about spirits and water. I found a site that said, "Water signifies the spiritual things of faith. . . . Water popularly represents life. It can be associated with birth, fertility, and refreshment. In a Christian context, water has many correlations. Christ walked on water and transmuted it into wine; thus, acts can be seen as a transcendence of the earthly condition. Christians are baptized with or in water, symbolizing a purification of the soul and an admission into the faith."

After meeting with Reverend Donna, I felt peace and comfort. She had identified and confirmed that I have a sixth sense. I believe that God instilled the sixth sense into my soul when I drowned and was brought back to life, and that part of God's mission that He gave me is to share my true-life experiences with others to help them understand that when a loved one dies, they never go away.

Years before Tony's death, I caught an interview Barbara Walters did with Patrick Swayze shortly after the release of the movie *Dirty Dancing* in 1987. The movie catapulted Patrick Swayze to stardom. Patrick had started taking dance lessons when he was two. His mother had been a dance instructor and choreographer. Patrick was one of the stars in her class. In his family, second best was not good enough, so he exceled in sports and dancing until an injury forced him to stop dancing, at which point he turned to acting.

His mother had taught him the meaning of discipline and told him that he could not expect life to be handed to him on a silver platter.

Although Patrick gained recognition with his acting, his heart told him that he still wanted to dance. He had numerous knee operations to correct his injury. That allowed him to audition for and land the lead role in *Dirty Dancing,* especially since he felt a strong connection to the lead character's personality. Patrick lived with quality, passion, and integrity.

When Patrick's father died in 1982, he struggled to accept his death, mainly because he had wanted to make his father proud and yet Patrick's greatest moments had come after his father's death.

Now during the interview, Barbara asked, "Are you sad that your father died before you became a superstar?"

"No," Patrick said. "There were times when I performed in high school and college and my father could not attend due to his work. Now that he has passed, I can have him with me anytime that I want."

Now that my parents and my husband had died, I thought back to this interview and smiled. It brought me comfort. And every time after that, whenever I have learned about the death of someone, I tell them about the Patrick Swayze interview. I find that they are grateful and appreciate hearing the story. I also suggest that they write in a journal to God and even write letters to loved ones who have passed.

But ultimately, as much as I wanted to hear the information from mediums, my Catholic faith began to convict me. I needed to trust God and His leadership in my life, not rely on what other humans were telling me. One day I turned to the Bible in search of God's message to His people and found Micah 5:12: "I will destroy your witchcraft and you will no longer cast spells."

In the process of getting closer to God, I made a commitment to eliminate mediums from my life. From that moment, I chose to follow God's chosen path and not rely on witchcraft. And I left the unanswered questions in God's hands.

Don't underestimate your family on the other side of the veil.
—Jeffrey K. Holland

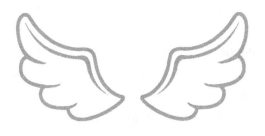

CHAPTER 8

HELPING HAND FROM GOD

Do not pray for an easy life; pray for the strength to endure a difficult one.
—Bruce Lee

One day I was driving when the song "Hello" by Lionel Richie came on the radio. It was my husband's and my favorite love song; it was "our" song. Even today, when I hear the music, my heart skips a beat.

The strange thing about anxiety attacks is that they can strike at any time. And one struck.

Even though I was driving, I was afraid to stop. I was sobbing uncontrollably and having trouble keeping the car on the road. One minute I felt perfectly fine; the next minute I was a basket case. The devil often attacks us without warning—primarily in our weakest moments.

My heart was pounding so hard that I felt as if I was having a heart attack. I felt smothered and began wheezing with an asthma attack. I searched for my inhaler and couldn't find it. I started to panic, which just made everything worse.

I had never encountered this kind of feeling before. It was terrifying.

"Please, God, help me!" I cried out. "I don't know what to do. I am scared and afraid I may hurt myself." And then the weight of everything came down on me. "I cannot bear to live one more day. God, where are You?"

Without warning, my car stopped, and I found myself sitting in my church's parking lot. I have no idea how I got there. But there I sat, staring at the church and rectory through tear-stained eyes, feeling uncertain of my next step.

It took me more than one hour to gain strength and to get out of my car. I started walking toward the church to pray, but God led me to the rectory's front door. I banged on the door like a crazy woman, as tears came again.

"Help me now! Help me now! I need to talk to a priest."

"I am sorry," the receptionist said. "But no one is available to help you. You will have to make an appointment."

I collapsed on the doorstep.

"Help!" the receptionist yelled and came to me.

Monsignor Lemon, who was preparing to leave for an appointment, came to the door and immediately knelt to assist me. "Cancel my appointment, please," he asked the receptionist, and led me into his office.

For the next three hours, Monsignor Lemon listened, consoled, and counseled me. I felt like I had a direct line to God, and I was an audience of one.

Thank You, God, for answering my prayer. I had cried out to Him, and He immediately answered. My faith strengthened, as I began to recognize God's incredible powers. And I felt hope settled into my soul.

I knew in my heart that I needed to forget the past, appreciate what remained, and look forward to what was coming next. *God, I pray that You are riding in the seat next to me on this roller coaster ride You call life.* He had to be; I would not survive without Him on my side.

"Would you consider changing your faith to the Catholic religion?" Monsignor Lemon asked.

I had been baptized a Baptist when I was a young girl, and I had been practicing Catholicism for many years with my husband, but I had never officially converted.

"We will start RCIA classes soon"—Rite of Christian Initiation of Adults. "I'm not saying you must convert to Catholicism, but it's a good place to start."

I agreed. It was time for me to make a commitment on my own and not just tag along because of my husband.

The first meeting I joined with eleven other people who were also considering becoming a Catholic. We introduced ourselves and spoke about why we were there. I quickly realized that we all had personal reasons for choosing to seek God and His incredible powers. For the first time in a long time, I felt safe from the outside world's trials.

I felt genuine sincerity from my classmates as I told my story and listened to theirs. Many of us were broken. We had attempted to repair ourselves independently, without success, and now turned to God for His help and strength.

I was amazed as I listened to experienced teachers who had a strong faith, had deep biblical knowledge, and truly lived each day with respect for God's presence.

Leaving that first meeting, I felt my healing begin—I knew I was in the right place for my soul to find peace.

As I continued attending the classes, I discovered that life is a journey that continually searches for meaning and purpose. I needed to turn my pain into a cause. I needed to turn my lemons into lemonade. But most important I found that when we turn our pain and disappointments over to God, we heal faster and become stronger.

We experience spiritual growth when we share God's wisdom. The human heart pangs of hunger for relationships that nurture one's maturity to love and be loved. We come to realize that something is missing in our lives and that something begins with God.

First, we must acknowledge that missing piece within ourselves. Unfortunately, for too long, Janet had been nowhere to be found. Edgar Allan Poe said it best: "I remained too much inside my head and ended up losing my mind."

I discovered that studying God's Word will lead to a better understanding of how God can help us heal. I found that when we commit our lives to God, we experience and recognize more miracles. As Job 5:9 states, "He performs wonders that cannot be fathomed, miracles that cannot be counted." But if our eyes are not wide open, we will not be able to see.

But when we seek God and open our eyes to new possibilities and allow ourselves to hope and dream, miracles abound the more. We will view our obstacles as opportunities to grow. We will discover that God chose us to grow and heal *through our pain* to be a more credible witness to help others get through their grief.

But oh, how quickly I could forget! One day I found myself lying in a fetal position on my bedroom floor, extremely angry, and having multiple panic attacks. I lay weakly on the floor for hours, only able to crawl like a snake to the bathroom to vomit. I had already wet my pants and honestly did not care. I crawled back to my bedroom floor with dried vomit on my face and smelling of urine. With no strength to move, I returned to my fetal position.

I found myself screaming at the top of my lungs, "God, where are You? I beg You. Please take away my pain!" And when He didn't answer right away, I wondered, *Where is God when I need Him most?*

The day turned into night, and the night turned sideways and upside down. I did not have a clue how I was going to survive. Once again, I felt lost and unable to imagine how or if I was going to heal.

I managed to crawl my way to a chaise lounge in my bedroom corner and curl into it. Slowly I picked up the remote control and switched on the television. It was 3:00 a.m. While flipping channels, I heard a woman preacher with a loud voice say, "Why are you sitting there feeling sorry for yourself? It does not matter who hurt you. You are responsible for your happiness."

My finger moved off the remote. This woman was speaking directly to me. I hit the guide on the television to find out who this was. Her name was Joyce Meyer.

She told me that I had two choices: "You can feel sorry for yourself and your circumstances, or you can choose to have a better life through hope, faith, prayer, and actions."

I knew she was right. So I began to pray. But instead of asking God to take away my pain, I asked Him for strength. I knew I also needed to pray for faith, hope, peace, forgiveness, love, understanding, gratefulness, among many other things. I knew that my soul needed time to heal. And that it was going to be a journey of steps forward and backward. But I felt confident that God would introduce more into my life when I was ready to receive it.

After I prayed, I set small daily goals to better myself. The first was to reduce the sleeping and antianxiety drugs I had been taking. Slowly, peace settled into my heart. There was no question that God was with me and answered my prayers at precisely the right moment. If He had responded when I was out of control and screaming for help, my heart would not have been opened to receive it. It would have been too quick a fix, which meant it wouldn't have lasted. But God's timing is always perfect. I had to choose to trust.

It was my husband's choice to die. Now it is my choice to live.

So I committed to taking baby steps and waiting patiently for God to put the pieces of my life's puzzle into place.

The next day I visited a bookstore and bought several Joyce Meyer books. I resonated with her down-to-earth tone and message as I read. She was very vulnerable, sharing that she'd had a terrible childhood and had been sexually abused by her father and other relatives until she was sixteen years old when she finally said, "No more!"

Joyce found God and fell in love with His teachings, knowing that she would not be where she was without Him. The more I read, the more she inspired me to turn my pain into purpose.

Later that night, God provided me with more inspiration. I saw an infomercial with Tony Robbins on television in which he was selling *Personal Power II—The Driving Force*. What interested me about Tony's program was that it was a thirty-day program designed for "Unlimited Success." I knew I was incapable of committing to something long term; however, I was not afraid to commit to something for thirty days.

Tony shared how he had hit rock bottom, living in his car, when a dream entered his heart. He knew that the only way to be successful was to read every book he could on self-improvement and apply what he learned. He discovered that success came by educating himself and then helping others to succeed by helping them understand that their powers lie within themselves.

"Are you working through challenges in your life and are open to working with the best?" Tony said. "This program is designed to empower you to take back control of your life and make the changes that will transform you from ordinary to extraordinary."

That was all I needed to hear. I picked up the phone and ordered.

When the tapes arrived, I set another baby-step goal to listen to a tape each day and do my best to apply what I had learned. Each session ended with a homework assignment to write in a journal by answering questions.

Day 1's session was "The Key to Personal Power." That day had two questions.

I read the first one out loud. "What two decisions have I been putting off, which, when I make them now, I will change my life?" I thought for a moment, then wrote, "Stop feeling sorry for myself. Stop thinking about my husband's betrayals and move on."

I moved to the second question: "What three different things can I do immediately that will be consistent with my two decisions?" Again I thought and then wrote, "(1) Start writing in a journal to release my thoughts, anger, and disappointments. (2) Start eating nutritiously and walking every day. (3) Start each day by reading a positive quotation and affirmation."

Sitting back, I put down my pen and thanked God again for how he'd led me to the messages from Joyce Meyer and Tony Robbins. Once again, I had cried out for help, and God answered my prayers. But thinking about these two people and their influence made me wonder, *Has God been trying to talk to me on other occasions through other ordinary people, but I did not recognize His help? Could my healing have started sooner, but I was too stubborn to open my eyes to see or my ears to hear?*

A statement I heard Joyce Meyer say sprang to my mind, *"There are no limitations in God's world."*

Can that possibly be true?

Ever since I was a child, people made fun of me, accusing me of being a dreamer. Despite their criticism, I continued to have big dreams though I kept them mostly to myself. But God seemed to be saying to my heart that He saw more in me than I ever saw in myself. That my "big" dreams weren't anything as big as the dreams He had for me—for all of us.

Even though I wanted to believe Joyce Meyer, I questioned whether her message was for real. I wanted to discover the truth for myself, so I turned to the Bible for my own confirmation. I had learned my lesson with the mediums that whatever I did, I needed to follow God's leading—and the best way to do that was to find out directly what He had to say—and that was by reading the Bible. As I searched through God's Word, I landed in the Old Testament, in the book of 1 Chronicles.

There it told the very brief story of a man named Jabez and the prayer he offered: "Oh, that You would bless me indeed, and enlarge my territory, that Your hand would be with me, and that You would keep me from evil, that I may not cause pain!" (1 Chronicles 4:10, nkjv). And the Bible said very simply that "God granted him what he requested."

This was the strength and hope I needed for a better tomorrow. And so I added to my list of baby-step goals to say the prayer every day and throughout each day.

I was so amazed by what is called the prayer of Jabez, that I searched online to find out more about it. I found an article on Crosswalk.com, "The Prayer of Jabez: 5 Inspiring Lessons." It definitely inspired me! The author wrote:

> When you pray, begin by acknowledging who God is! . . . When you pray, do it with a heart fully invested in the blessings of God. . . . When you pray, ask God to multiply your territory and do more through you! . . . When you pray, request more than blessings and provision but that God's hand would lead you through any circumstances and trials that come your way. That is the greatest blessing. . . . When you pray, come to God vulnerable and ready for Him to turn your weaknesses into His glory.

It got me thinking about the many times in the past God had placed opportunities to "expand my territory." Two years before Tony died, he walked into our bathroom, where I was putting on makeup, and declared, "You are going to write a book one day."

"Where did that statement come from?" I asked.

He shrugged. "I don't know. I just felt compelled to say it." Then he turned and walked away.

My husband sowed a seed inside my mind and spirit. I had no idea that my driving force would be propelled by my desperate need to find myself, find inner peace, and strive to help others get through their pain. But God knew.

It's incredible how God draws upon ordinary people in our lives to plant seeds of quests, encouragement, love, and more. He planted a seed in me back then to write this book, and I had no idea at the time that He was preparing me to expand my territory. It didn't matter that I was in Mr. Fox's remedial reading class in the seventh grade, or that my writing and reading skills growing up weren't strong enough to gain great attention. Plenty of other people had much better writing qualifications! But God works differently from how we view things. When God expands our territory, it isn't about our skill but about His will.

And so, if God chose me for this mission, I was not going to disappoint Him. That became another baby-step goal: to write my experiences and lessons learned. Whether it remained in a journal or got published, I would show up and write, and God would open the doors as He saw fit.

Not long after I began my recovery, my sister Diane sent me a card of encouragement. She told me that she loved me, assured me that everything would be okay, and wrote, "Take baby steps, just like Mackenzie."

My granddaughter, Mackenzie, was nine months old and starting to walk. Her message—really, God's message—to me got me through many difficult times. When I felt myself falling into despair, I would whisper those words. "Take baby steps."

I created a plan to be the best person I could be to live my best life. I knew becoming the best person wasn't just for my own healing—it was then to reach beyond myself to help others. But I had to gain much wisdom and go through much pain to heal appropriately before allowing myself to help others get through their grief. It would feel disingenuous to try to help others when I wasn't in a healthy place.

In addition to reading and learning from Joyce Meyer and Tony Robbins, I had the opportunity to go on a "Success at Sea" cruise with Zig Ziglar, a man whose every word was positive. Before the cruise, I decided to prepare myself mentally, so I read many of Zig's books. He was well-known for his stories. Like Jesus, Zig spoke in parables to teach people.

I fell in love with his teachings and discovered that Zig was a man of faith who truly believed in God and His incredible powers. Zig credited all his success to God. And his life story was incredible.

Growing up, his family was impoverished. He was the tenth of twelve children. His father died from a stroke when Zig was six years old, and his younger sister died two days later. In 2007, at the age of eighty-one, Zig fell down a flight of stairs that left him with short-term memory problems. Even with his disability, he traveled around the world, continuing with his motivational speaking. Nothing was going to stop Zig.

Since I'd made a commitment to read inspiring quotations every day, I found myself reading many of his. They gave me hope when I felt hopeless; they reminded me that "failure is an event, not a person," and they permitted me to think of myself as a winner. But to see myself as a winner, I needed to "plan to win, prepare to win, and expect to win," as he often told his audiences. As I read significant quotes from him, I wrote them down in my journal. One in particular made a strong impression upon me: "You don't have to be great at something to start, but you have to start to be great at something."

By the time the cruise came around, I was set and ready to go!

I had a wonderful time, learning and relaxing and meeting other people who were encouraging. One such person was a wild and crazy guy named Florian who was co-owner of a hedge fund. He was from Zurich, Switzerland. He had three children, was single, had homes in Paris, Monaco, Munich, and of course Zurich. He was also a very handsome model, a professional race-car driver, and spoke seven languages fluently.

After the cruise, I flew to Zurich and spent two weeks with Florian and his family. Even though it was part of my running away, I needed to get serious about making money. I was spending more than I was making, and that was leading to self-destruction.

I found that I could run, but I couldn't outrun my troubles. While in Zurich, one morning I woke up to the reality of Tony's death, the circumstances surrounding it, and my unknown future staring me in the face. It terrified me. For hours I lay on the hotel floor in a fetal position, rocking myself back and forth. Even though I had vowed to discontinue taking anxiety pills, I packed a bottle for peace of mind . . . for just in case. Because I felt like I was having an out-of-body experience, I took several anxiety pills to calm me down.

I fell asleep and woke up eight hours later. I was not sure how I would be able to endure one more day.

Even though I had made great strides in my grief and healing, with God's help, I realized that healing doesn't take a linear path. Grief and anger can pop up at any time—and it did in full force. I was furious with Tony and what he had done. Even though I knew in my heart that negative thinking and hatred solved nothing, and destroyed everything, I still wanted to be mad at the way he had put me in this position. The pain was too great to bear.

"God, I need Your peace and strength to help me get through this."

I remembered that my therapist told me that *anger* was one letter short of *danger*. She'd also told me that Buddha said, "To be angry is to let others' mistakes punish yourself" and "Holding onto anger is like drinking poison and expecting the other person to die."

Determination helped me pull myself together.

"Today is the day that I am going to forgive Tony," I told myself.

I dressed and ventured out to find a Catholic church. Finally, not far from the hotel I found the Liebfrauenkirche—a beautiful Catholic church built in 1893.

I timidly entered the building and was greeted by a nun who appeared to be about twenty-five years old and spoke only German. I smiled and nodded then walked farther in, where I encountered a life-sized marble statue of the Pieta (Virgin Mary holding her son Jesus).

It's impressive that Michelangelo sculpted the original statue in his early twenties. Carved in 1498–1499, it is the only sculpture Michelangelo ever signed.

As I stood facing it, my mind went back to the trip Tony and I had taken only a couple years before when we'd enjoyed a wine tour through Italy. We'd toured the Vatican and viewed the original sculpture there.

I swallowed my tears and walked down the main aisle of the church until I stepped into a row about ten feet from the sculpture. I pulled out the kneeler and knelt, where I prayed for a long time before I could muster myself to sit in a pew. A million thoughts rushed through my mind. One moment I seemed to be in total control. The next moment, my mind wandered everywhere but in the present.

I am not sure where I found the strength to walk again. As I finally approached the door to leave, the nun approached me. "Bist du in Ordnung? Kann ich lhnen mit irgendwas helfen?" Though I couldn't understand what she was saying, I got the gist: "Are you all right? Can I help you with anything?"

I began crying so hard, I could barely speak. I was certain I was having a nervous breakdown.

"Where can I buy rosaries?" I asked and held my hand as though I was holding one.

She shook her head, clearly not understanding what I was saying and spoke something, which I clearly didn't understand. Finally, our game of charades connected, and she smiled kindly. She took hers, a simple wooden rosary, which hung from her sash, and held it out for me to take.

"Oh, no no, I can't take your rosary," I told her, shaking my head to communicate.

But she nodded just as fiercely.

I insisted that I could not take them, and she insisted more. When I realized she wouldn't allow me to refuse, I opened my hands and received her sacrificial gift, which she placed gently in my hands.

I looked down at the carved wooden beads strung on cotton cord. Thousands of prayers had graced each bead before she'd gifted it to me. Of all the things I owned, I knew immediately that this rosary would be one of my most cherished possessions. Her unselfish act of kindness was more than a miracle to me. Once again, I saw God's hand comforting me and showing me that He creates miracles through ordinary people.

She took me under her arms like an angel giving protection and told me her name was Sister Ariane. Then in broken English, she asked if I would like to speak to a priest. I was hesitant to take up any more of her time. But once again she insisted, and we walked to the rectory in search of the one priest who spoke English. He was not available, so the receptionist took my phone number, and promised to pass it along to him. He called at 11:00 p.m. that night.

We spoke for three hours on the phone. I listened intently to his encouraging words of wisdom. He explained to me that when we forgive someone, we are not excusing the act. He helped me see that forgiving Tony was the only way to free my mind and body from the pain.

And so, on that day, nearly three years after his death, I forgave my husband. I forgave him for the pain and suffering he caused me—nothing more and nothing less. And my healing process began once more.

Forgiveness, just like healing, takes time and a commitment that I had to renew regularly.

After I said goodbye to the priest, I was too wide awake to go to sleep, so I randomly opened the Bible. God knows what to say with perfect timing, and He led me to a passage in Romans: "We know that God causes all things to work together for good to those who love God, to those who are called according to His purpose" (8:28, nasb).

I decided to spend the balance of my trip reading the Bible and looking for passages that would help me better understand the process of forgiveness. Saying that I was going to forgive and practicing the actual act of forgiving was a challenging task. As much as I wanted to be positive, I found myself constantly thinking about the negatives. I noticed that my demeanor changed for the worse when I had negative thoughts.

Out of survival, if a negative thought entered my mind, I made a firm commitment to immediately change my way of thinking. This one act gave me the courage to overcome anything negative that entered my life. I looked for an opportunity in each negative situation and always found something better.

I felt it necessary not to put a time stamp in place for permission to move forward. Instead, I had surrendered my life to God and now I asked Him for guidance. God directed me to Matthew 6:14-15: "If you forgive other people when they sin against you, your heavenly Father will also forgive you. But if you do not forgive others their sins, your Father will not forgive your sins."

God has a bigger plan with no limitations, I reminded myself.

Converting to Catholicism is a serious and committed process, which I embraced. Days before becoming a Catholic, I attended a mass where Bishop Michael Saltarelli, the bishop of the Wilmington diocese, was speaking. He gave a very compelling sermon on Romans 5:20: "The law entered that the offense might abound. But where sin abounded, grace abounded much more" (nkjv).

A reception followed the mass for incoming Catholics. After the mass, I was the first in line to meet the bishop.

He took my hands and secured them tightly with his own and would not let go. I felt the power of God's hands holding my hands through the bishop.

"Did you hear what I said in my sermon?" he asked.

"Yes."

He squeezed my hands slightly. "Did you understand my message?"

I was surprised that he asked me again. "I think I did."

"Sins abound. God's grace abounds the more." His message was straightforward and biblical.

God is telling me not to worry about the sins and injustices that were surrounding me through everything I've had to endure, I thought. *God is watching over me, and God's grace will protect me.*

Later that day, as I recalled the scene with the bishop, I asked God, "How will I ever trust again?"

He answered by directing me to Proverbs 3:5-6: "Trust in the Lord with all your heart and lean not on your own understanding; in all your ways submit to him, and he will make your paths straight."

I read the words again and then closed my eyes and repeated the words now burned into my brain. I had no understanding of my past, my present, or my future. But God's Word was encouraging me to trust Him, because He would faithfully lead me where I needed to go.

As I continued to read passages that comforted me, I thirsted for more. I purchased a journal and began writing Bible passages in it. I also wrote positive statements, quotations, and interesting positive lines from magazines and television shows.

While shuffling through a box of miscellaneous papers, I found a business card for a grief counselor. A couple years before, while getting a much-needed massage, my massage therapist gave me the counselor's card, encouraging me to make an appointment.

"She's amazing at helping people recover after a tragic loss," she'd told me.

Now finding the card, I gave the grief counselor, named Karen Covey Moore, a call and set up an appointment.

As it turned out, both Karen's mother and son committed suicide. She was the first person I spoke to who truly knew how I felt.

"Do you write in a journal?" she asked.

I proudly sat up in my chair. "Yes."

"When you write in a journal, do you write directly to God?"

I was stunned by the question. "I never thought to do that. You mean, I can write directly to God?"

"Of course!" she said.

"Thank you!" I told her. "You have taken me to a place where I've never been before. I know your suggestion will help me heal faster as I get closer to God."

Before leaving, I sat in a chair and cried, amazed yet again by God's faithfulness. *God is directing me to the right people. I wonder what other surprises He has in store for me?*

Karen took me into her arms and hugged me. "Remember, God is with you always. He allows you to fall so that when you rise, you will have a greater strength and better understanding."

I drove directly to a bookstore and purchased a thin bound journal to write my letters to God. It was important to me to choose a thin and bound journal, since I did not know how strong my commitment would be and did not want to be overwhelmed with a large journal. I also did not want to haphazardly tear out pages when I became frustrated.

On May 7, 2004, while sitting in perpetual adoration at my church, I pulled out my journal and began to write.

Dear God,

Hear my prayers. First, let me say, thank You. Thank You for the joys in my life and also for the pain. I did not realize that I am supposed to thank You for my pain. Yesterday Monsignor Lemon told me, "We must all walk the journey that God has for our lives, and God promises that there is purpose in all pain."

He told me, "God loves us and wants to use the hurt and pain in our world to bring Him glory."

As You know, after Tony died, I experienced more pain than I thought any one person could bear. I realized that You were the only one I could turn to for help. It seems like I ask You for help every day. I hope You don't mind my asking.

I have many fears in life. My greatest fear is living the rest of my life alone. I realize that my greatest inner strength has come to me over the past two years and I know that I needed to go through the pain to give me a better understanding of You and of myself.

Every day when I wake up, I still have pain in my heart. I feel that in the area of being loved unconditionally without any thought of betrayal, I have been overlooked. Okay, I hear what You are saying. My heart has to fully heal before I can entertain the possibility of looking for love.

I do not like feeling this way. It is tearing me up inside. Please, I beg of You, heal my heart of this pain and help me get focused on other areas in my life so I have something good to look forward to each day.

Normally, I am a very optimistic person. I memorized Jeremiah 29:11: "'I know the plans I have for you,' declares the Lord, 'plans to prosper you and not to harm you, plans to give you hope and a future.'" I know that You are in control and have great plans for me. I will hold that promise close to my heart with faith, hope, and expectation.

Love,

Janet

One day I got down on my knees and prayed for God to take away my pain once again. I prayed that He would give me something I could become passionate about. Within days I received a compelling message from Him.

On June 18, 2004, I wondered what God would say to me, so I asked God to write a letter to me.

I headed the page "Dear Janet," and signed the bottom, "Love, God." Empty lines waited patiently while I sat anxiously to see if my request was foolish or profound.

Almost thirty minutes passed when my hand started to write.

Dear Janet,

I look at you and see a beautiful woman who is still a little confused about herself, how you will live your life, and when it's going to end. My precious child, you worry too much. Now that our relationship is growing closer, know that you can stop worrying about your future.

I plan to have you live for a long time and to be healthy. You see, you are one of the chosen ones I selected to make a difference in this world. You smile a lot and bring much happiness to many people's lives, even when you only touch their lives for a moment. I have great plans for you.

Read and study the Bible. There you will find My promises. Know that whatever I did for others, I will do for you. One promise can be found in Psalm 32:8: "I will guide you along the best pathway for your life. I will advise you and watch over you."

Revisit the miracles that I have placed in your life. Tell others about My amazing works. Tell them to believe in Me and they will experience blessings in their lives too.

You and I both know that "with Me," all is wonderful. "Without Me," life can be a living hell.

The only way to keep the devil out of your life is to be closer to Me. I will protect all, and I will give safe harbor to all who come to Me for help and seek My guidance.

You are a grand treasure to Me. Please remember that you will find true love, and everything will be more than just okay.

Love,

God

Today, I still face many challenges. I have no fears, what so ever. I have learned to let go of many things that I can see. My heart continually tells me that God has many reasons for removing items from our lives. Today, God is giving me a glimpse of my future. It is more significant than I could ever have imagined. Amazing God!

Am I afraid? Sometimes. I am moving out of my comfort zone. The funny part is that God is always giving me signals to move forward. When I am afraid to move forward on my own, God steps in and decides for me.

At first, I had anxiety attacks and the pain of disappointment, wondering why and how I would move forward, not knowing where I was going.

One day I was searching online for inspiring quotes and I came across a beautiful poem, titled "Stepping Stones," written by an anonymous author.

The Lord came to me like a dream one day
And asked, Why do you sorrow?
I answered, Lord, my life is so full of pain,
I can't face one more tomorrow.

The Lord sat down beside me
And gently took my hand.
He said, Let me explain to you,
And then you'll understand.
Each sorrow is a stepping stone
You must surmount each day,
And every stepping stone you climb
Is a sorrow that's passed away.

The road of life is a mountainside,
With crevices in which to be caught,
But as you struggle on your way,
I the Rock will lend support.

Every stepping stone you climb
Makes spirit and heart grow strong.
Exercising character and faith,
This road seems painful and long.

The way is paved with stepping stones,
To uplift your heart and soul,
Though difficult, they aid your way,
To a City paved with gold.

I know that you are tired,
For I too have walked this way.
My sorrows did they multiply,

But I cleared many stones away.

I left my rock to lift you up,
I left behind my story.
To give you strength to make your climb,
To that special place in glory.

And never fear, the Rock is here,
You'll never climb this mountain alone.
Surmount life's sorrows, continue on,
For they are but stepping stones.

I smiled as I thought about the past three years. I'd been through so much, but now as I thought about it all, I realized that was exactly how God had been leading me. I'd been making baby-step goals, and they were all stepping stones.

Later that night, I opened my Bible and read Psalm 55. I stopped when landed at verse 22: "Cast your cares on the Lord and He will sustain you; He will never let the righteous be shaken." I looked it up in a different transition and read it: "Give your burdens to the Lord, and He will take care of you. He will not permit the godly to slip and fall" (nlt).

I knew His Word was true. "Thank You, God," I prayed.

I found that the more open I became to listening to and hearing from God, the more He spoke. As C. S. Lewis wrote in *The Problem of Pain*, "God whispers to us in our pleasures, speaks in our conscience, but shouts in our pain." As terrible as my experience had been with losing Tony and the circumstances by which it happened, and then discovering so many secrets, I was grateful that God had shouted in my pain to get my attention and to draw me closer to Him. That's where I truly found comfort, peace, and blessings.

One evening I watched *The Wizard of Oz* on television, a movie I'd loved since childhood. In the movie, Dorothy is swept up in her house by a tornado and lands in Oz, directly on top of the Wicked Witch of the East, killing her. Glinda, the Good Witch of the North, thanked Dorothy for saving the Munchkins from the evil witch's tyranny.

Though appreciative, Dorothy only wanted to go back home to Kansas. Glinda told Dorothy that the only way she would return home would be to see the Wizard of Oz so that he could grant her wish. Then she magically transferred the dead witch's ruby slippers onto Dorothy's feet.

To get to the Wizard, Dorothy had to follow the Yellow Brick Road. Along the way, Dorothy met a Scarecrow, a Lion, and a Tin Man, who were looking for a brain, courage, and a heart, respectively. So they traveled with her. They thought, undoubtedly, the great and powerful Wizard could also provide a brain, courage, and a heart.

But once they arrived and met with the Wizard, he confessed that he was not powerful enough to grant their wishes. However, he gave the Scarecrow a diploma, the Tin Man a ticking clock in the shape of a heart, and the lion a medal of courage.

He agreed to take Dorothy back to Kansas in a hot air balloon, but after Dorothy's dog, Toto, escaped from her arms, she jumped out of the basket to retrieve him. It was too late. The ropes that tied down the balloon loosened, and it flew away.

Glinda pointed to the ruby slippers and told Dorothy that she had the power to return home. Glinda had never told Dorothy how powerful the slippers were. If Glinda had granted Dorothy her wish when she asked, the young girl would not have appreciated her home as much as she did in the end.

She would never have met the Scarecrow, the Tin Man, and the Lion, who showed her that she also needed wisdom, courage, and love to solve her problems. And she never would have experienced victory over wickedness or learned to demonstrate her power to solve her problems. She would not have realized that sometimes the solution to a problem is straightforward, and that she already possessed the power. She just needed to believe in herself.

Those were all things I needed to learn and remember as well. As Oprah Winfrey has said, "Everything happens for a reason, even when we are not wise enough to see it. When there is no struggle, there is no strength."

I had experienced the struggle. And now slowly I was experiencing the strength.

There is no better way to thank God for your sight
than by giving a helping hand to someone in the dark.
—Helen Keller

CHAPTER 9

THERE IS A TIME FOR EVERYTHING

Never mistake knowledge for wisdom. One helps you make a living;
the other helps you make a life.
—Sandra Carey

Ever since I became a Catholic, I decided to create a journey for my life and faith that was mine to embrace rather than accepting the faith because it was my husband's and his family's. Once I did that, I found myself thirsting for more of God's Word. Not just reading His Word, but dissecting it to see how the words written thousands of years ago applied to my life today.

If there was one thing I had learned through this entire experience with Tony's death and the aftermath was that the time frame for people healing is a direct correlation of how they interact with God. I had a love-hate relationship with God right after my husband died. Looking back, I discovered my life started changing for the better when I surrendered the whole of myself to God.

I knew that I was continually taking one step forward and two steps backward since Tony's passing. I knew that something had to change dramatically, or I would remain a victim of my life circumstances.

What do I need to do to turn my life around and become victorious? I wondered, and one day I turned to the Bible to seek answers and search for a way to understand God a little better and to learn how God could help me. I randomly opened the Bible and found myself reading a well-known passage:

> There is a time for everything,
> and a season for every activity under the heavens:
> a time to be born and a time to die,
> a time to plant, and a time to uproot,
> a time to kill and a time to heal,
> a time to tear down and a time to build,
> a time to weep and a time to laugh,
> a time to mourn, and a time to dance,
> a time to scatter stones and a time to gather them,
> a time to embrace and a time to refrain from embracing,
> a time to search and a time to give up,
> a time to keep and a time to throw away,
> a time to tear and a time to mend,
> a time to be silent and a time to speak,
> a time to love and a time to hate,
> a time for war and a time for peace. (Ecclesiastes 3:1-8)

I sat back and began to reflect on all the different seasons this passage was referring to. I could relate on many levels. For the next hour or so, I broke down each season and jotted my thoughts about it into my journal.

"A time to be born."

When Tony died, I felt like a part of me died with him. And for a while, that's how I have lived. But figuratively stepping outside of my body to view my life circumstances without judgment or emotion has made me realize that I am looking at a pathetic woman with no hope for a future. I have viewed myself as a victim of my circumstances. But no more. I heard about people being reborn, in which they found a new purpose for their pain that allowed them to live again. It is time for me to be born. My first step in that process is to make God part of my everyday life, asking for His help to allow me to grow strong.

"A time to die."

Much of my past has to die—mostly the negatives, the anger, and the memory of betrayals. If I am going to heal myself with God's help, I need to let go of the things that hurt me.

"A time to plant."

I know that I need to believe in God for the seed before believing in the harvest. I understand that the harvest is everything that we keep, and the seed is anything that we sow. We can have no reward or harvest until we plant a seed and labor over it. My tears have long been seeds, but I believe those seeds will reap joy. Planting seeds requires much patience, wisdom, understanding, and the ability to visualize the harvest that is to come in God's timing.

"A time to uproot."

My husband and I lived in the same location for thirteen years. I am living among the memories. It is tough when you are settled in one place to uproot completely. *Is it time for me to move?* I cannot decide on my own; I need to pray for God to give me a sign when He feels it is time to go.

"A time to kill."
Not in a literal sense. However, the thought crossed my mind for a minute or two to kill the people trying to destroy me. That "crazy" thought was a slap across my face and made me take a step backward. Negative thoughts will do nothing but destroy me and my mind. I see now that anger has been destroying me from the inside out.

"A time to heal."
Today and every day, I feel like I am healing myself. Each day has many challenges. I have learned to turn to God with a prayer to speed my recovery. My only regret is that I did not ask God for His help sooner.

"A time to tear down."
As I look at the people around me, I have seen that I have ten people who are helping me stand tall for every person who is trying to tear me down. I need to tear down those relationships and remove all negative people from my life. Their negativity will only make me question myself about my ability to change my life and move on into health.

"A time to build."
I have made a firm commitment to start building on my dreams. I know that if I do not put myself first, I cannot someday help someone else build their dreams. I have created a vision board and cut out pictures of the dreams for my future. Included is meeting new people and helping them find hope and a new purpose for their lives.

"A time to weep."

Now and then, I regret that I have been so naïve. On the one hand, I feel the need to weep, because my husband robbed me of sixteen years of my life that I could have spent with someone else who hopefully would have been loving, kind, and loyal. On the other hand, if my husband were not the deceitful person he was, I probably would never have embraced my faith.

"A time to laugh."

I laugh every day with my family and friends. They are amazing! I laugh at myself, because I tend to be a little clumsy. It's okay and good for my health and sanity to laugh!

"A time to mourn."

I know that grief never ends. Grief is not a sign of weakness, nor is it a lack of faith. It is the price of love. One of the worst parts about grief is that the person I need to talk to the most is the one who is no longer here. So I don't need to apologize for grieving—or for taking as long as I need, knowing that may be different from how long someone else thinks I should grieve.

"A time to dance."

Someone said it best: "We are the dancers; we create the dreams." Dancing is magical. It's an action that sets me free, that allows me to take my mind off the negatives. Sometimes it's good just to turn on some music and move.

"A time to scatter stones."

I feel I am scattering stones every day. I've heard it said, "I alone cannot change the world, but I can cast a stone across the waters to create many ripples."

"A time to gather stones."

I am collecting the stones that people have thrown at me and choose not to throw them back. I am collecting them and using them as stepping stones to strengthen and rebuild my life.

"A time to embrace."

I am embracing my faith and I strive every day to embrace my life each day, aiming to become a better version of myself.

"A time to refrain from embracing."

I choose to refrain from embracing anything negative, including people who do not want the best for me. I will not allow anyone in my life who cause me pain, no matter who they are.

"A time to search."

I find myself searching for God, recognizing His incredible powers every day. Thirteenth-century Persian poet Rumi said it best: "I searched for God and found only myself. I searched for myself and found only God."

"A time to give up."

I have given up on trying to be perfect, and I am more accepting of myself. As Harriet Beecher Stowe said, "Never give up, for that is just the place and time that the tide will turn."

"A time to keep."

Regarding feelings about my husband, I have decided to remember only the good and toss away the bad memories. When I focus on the goodness, the good memories, I feel stronger and more at peace.

"A time to throw away."

When I was forced to file for bankruptcy and lose my home of twenty-three years, because of the financial mess I found myself in after Tony's death, I had to throw away many things. It broke my heart to part with those treasured things, however, the presence of their existence reminded me of all the joint ventures I experienced with my husband. Those things can't bring my husband or our life together back. Holding onto them will only hold me back and keep me from moving on and healing.

"A time to tear."

Too often I have torn myself apart to keep myself together. Many times, I have wondered if I am good enough or brave enough to make it through to the next day. I have attempted to repair myself without assistance, which has only led to self-destruction.

"A time to mend."

I choose to mend the broken things in my life only if I feel they are worth saving.

God's grace is the glue to repair my broken soul. With God's help, I can take the broken pieces of my life and use them to create a new piece of art.

"A time to be silent."

Sometimes remaining silent—especially when everything within me wants to yell out my pain—can be a great source of strength. I have learned that the closer I come to the truth of my husband's wayward life, the more silent I have to become. When I remain silent, I can hear God's words of comfort and guidance, and I can trust that He will provide and avenge.

"A time to speak."

I choose my words more carefully and only speak after I listen intently. Being a better listener has made me realize that there are far better things ahead than anything we leave behind. Now is the time for me to speak to influence others and help change many lives.

"A time to love."

Today, I choose only to love. I have lived many years hating many people who hurt me. When I walked away, my hate for them went away too, and in its place, I am better able to love. Life is too short to live in the negative.

"A time to hate."

I hated what Tony had done to himself, to me, and to his friends and family. I hate how death can so easily steal someone I love.

"A time for war."

I have wrestled with the tragedy of the war between good and evil. I feel like I need to defeat evil in order to become victorious. And that is war. Unfortunately, as war so often does, it still leaves me heartbroken. I must commit to keep up the battle and fight for good and light and hope.

"A time for peace."

I am learning that the most significant path to inner peace is to ignore the things that upset me. As I have done that, I have discovered that I can find tranquility even during a storm. My inner peace begins the moment I choose not to allow another person or event to control my emotions.

I put down my pen and reread my thoughts and how I dug deeper into God's Word by dissecting what it meant and how I could apply it to my life. God used this passage to show me that if I was patient and tough enough, one day my pain would be useful to me. I hated living in this season of pain and grief, but this passage reminded me that seasons do not last forever. We must be patient with ourselves as we grieve and grow. We have much to learn to move on from our tragedies. We are all victims of something. That realization made me feel not so alone and encouraged me in the goal to go from *victims* to *victory* and to do whatever it takes to prepare myself so that when the season is over, I'm ready to begin the new season stronger.

Embrace this season of life, for it is just that . . . a season.
—Unknown

CHAPTER 10

HOW TO HEAL A BROKEN HEART IN THIRTY DAYS

Pain makes you stronger. Tears make you braver.
Heartbreak makes you wiser. Be grateful
for your past because it helped shape who you are.
And thank your past for a better future.
—Marc Chernoff

One day I visited a Barnes and Noble bookstore. There I found a book called, *How to Heal a Broken Heart in 30 Days: A Day-by-Day Guide to Saying Goodbye and Getting On with Your Life* by Howard Bronson and Mike Riley. I turned it over to read the back cover copy.

It's over. Now what? Suffering from a broken heart? Afraid you'll

143

never get over this feeling of emptiness and loss? You can, and with the help of this easy-to-follow program of action, you will.

Follow Howard Bronson and Mike Riley as they lead you through a thirty-day plan for recovering from your broken heart. They will guide you through a brief period of mourning for your loss, and then the process of rebuilding yourself and your life. You are encouraged to enjoy good memories of the relationship that's just ended, while remembering the reasons for the breakup. You will learn to take responsibility for your own emotions, face your fears, and ultimately to seek new people and new experiences. Find out:

- How and why to cry 'til dry.
- *Good* ways to beat loneliness.
- How to "let go" of old memories and resentments.

How to Heal a Broken Heart in 30 Days prescribes a wide array of tested and proven insights and exercises. After thirty days of active self-restoration, your heart will be healed and whole again—and you'll be ready for anything. Of course, your feelings of grief, hurt, or shame may come and go. But in less than a month, you can be ready to deal with life's new challenges. With positive sense of emotional balance, you may never have had before.

Intrigued, I purchased it, went home, and immediately began to read. Although the authors wrote the book to deal with the breakup of relationships, rather than the end of a relationship as a result of a death, I found the information valuable.

It seemed as though each page held a treasure trove of insight and information.

There are so many people who hurt beyond our wildest imagination.

We feel a total emptiness inside. We talk to many people in search of answers. However, in most cases, we do not know the questions to ask. The assistance we get is limited. People do not know how we feel, and we pray to God that they never will.

We soon realize that we are the only one responsible for our happiness and success. I found that I could not rely on others to help me; I had to help myself. If I tried very hard and disappointed myself, I would walk away and try something else. Many days I felt so overwhelmed that I did nothing. Now I eagerly anticipated what new insight I would gain from that book. I didn't have to wait long. They wrote:

Day 1
Independence: The Emotional Circus

Your first reaction to the end of your relationship is likely to be in shock. As soon as the shock wears off, grief arrives. Next, the whole emotional circus stirs: "I'm free. I'm relieved. Yet I'm devastated. I'm furious, hopeful, afraid." Your feelings may broaden into a multicolored panorama. They may include everything from the awesome sense of liberation you felt as a kid on the last day of school to the nightmare sense that you've just failed your final exam. Back and forth . . .

Please relax. For better and for worse, your liberation has arrived: it's your Independence Day. As soon as you can bear to share the news of the loss with friends and other loved ones, you're more than likely to find sympathetic support—for at least today.

But prepare yourself. Soon enough, though hopefully not on Day One of your recovery, some self-appointed Calvinist will remind you. You must work on yourself, or more primitively: You got to do the work. That's when dread may set in. Your precious relationship has just died, and now someone wants to sentence you to hard labor. Your reaction of dread will be deepened by the serious tones in which this grim advice is usually offered. At best, the work will sound like doing chores for Mom, as though you must take out all your emotional garbage. Phew!

Skeptics might well deny the need to do this "work." They'll say: The work? What work? I was in a romantic relationship for quite a while.

For much of that time, it was good and rewarding. Is the impulse to deny this "work" stuff something to feel guilty about? At the ultimate level of insight, you must always remember that you are whole and complete, a perfect person, destined to be just as you are.

Using the guidance of the authors of this book, your next thirty days will see you through a journey of self-recovery. You'll not be overloaded with new ideas about love and human nature. Instead, you'll be strengthened with no work at all. If you want to build your body's muscles, you go to the gym. You work out. Here, we offer a cerebral spa for your wounded emotions. It's designed to help you realize your will's healing strength and ability to reintegrate the pieces of your broken heart."

Day 1—Helpful Hurters

So, what about this "work" stuff that others talk about? How long do you have to do it? And why bother? As some people speak about it, this "work" sounds like a prison sentence.

All you did was lose or outgrow a love. Now you need to begin a new adventure of healing. Why should you have to do hard labor for this? The growing sense of confinement that such ideas of work may inspire could just add to your pain and confusion.

Everyone will seem eager to give you easy answers. Too

few of those answers will make complete and immediate sense. Your sole certainty is that you hurt, really hurt, right now. That which had once seemed comforting has been wrested away from you. You find yourself in murky darkness. You need strong, clear light, yet all those near you have to offer are candles and matches.

You're in a susceptible state. Sad songs make sense like never before. Whether you feel vindicated and defiant or defeated for all time, you may be wider open than usual, more vulnerable. Your friends and advisors may suggest that your broken spirit requires long-winded, obscure instructions about how to get through these difficult times.

If you ask for it, advice will arrive from all sides: via face-to-face contact, email, voicemail, or ordinary mail, even as rumors passed on the wind. There's so much advice out there; however, if you listen to all of it, your confusion will certainly deepen, and you may forget one simple fact. That's the trustworthy words of the good witch of Oz, which offer all the wisdom you'll ever need: "You had the power within you all along."

Your confusion with the advice you're being offered may be well-founded. Your advisors' motives may range from true generosity to barely concealed power plays. At best, people see offering advice to the afflicted as doing their good work, especially when it's easy to offer. And offering love advice to others who suffer makes us feel better about ourselves. Offering advice can also be a token in a contest for power, with the advisor really saying, "I'm better than you because I'm not suffering as you are. And I know how to get out of the trouble you're in. It's about time you followed my lead."

People who say, "I'm sorry, but I don't know what to tell you," might sound as though they really don't care. But they may be the most honest of all your advisors. Most of us want to help end the suffering of others, especially when it can be carried out in a mindless manner. So, we say: "You'll be all right"; "Men are like buses, there's a new one along every five minutes"; "You weren't right for each other": "There's plenty more fish in the sea": et cetera.

Day 1—Truth and Proof

The truth is no one knows what's best for you. And there's a very good reason for that. No one really understands your personal experience like you do.

Also, many of us have been taught to think that intimately loving someone is a complicated project. Such thinking can make the prospect of an enduring romantic relationship seem an unattainable task. It can seem so difficult, in fact, that some people may forgo love altogether, while others blindly and hopelessly leap into new relationships without pause for reflection. Or they may feel the pain of a failed relationship so profoundly that they fall into an extended depression—down so far that all advice sails right over their heads.

The information age has both its rewards and consequences. Every book, tape, or therapeutic seminar aspires to add to our knowledge base. The abundance of new data has potential benefits, but our progress can collapse from the immensity of its weight.

The purpose of this guide is to lighten that load. The words and exercises you will find here are designed to take the weight out of the work in the breakup process. What little "work" we do suggest is modest and can help you realize a wholeness you've never experienced before.

Some of your current advisors may view a breakup as being a kind of death. The erudite ones may even be able to break down your breakup into grid-like patterns, telling you of the phases you must go through to achieve peace and relational happiness once again.

Shock, anger, denial, bargaining, and resolution are the classic phases of grieving that attend a mortal loss. But what if you don't experience these feelings? Does that mean you haven't come to terms with the passage of a lover into your past? Of course not.

A breakup is not a death, except perhaps the death of one phase of your life or an illusion about love. And if you could correct that illusion in a short time, why should you then choose to stretch out the process?

This presents a problem. The pursuit of emotional healing for its own sake has become so popular in the past few decades that many people spend far more time working at healing (or clinging to wounds) than at living and loving. The results are not always productive. Look at that angry person who spends all his time blaming you, people like you, or even people like his parents, for all his miseries. Beware of counsel that your recovery should involve a long, drawn-out, and often expensive process.

The unhappy end of an intimate relationship can generate some of the ugliest ironies you will ever experience. Get ready. The person you loved, held, and cared for, and were most intimate with, is now nothing but a fragile set of memories that will vanish into the mists of the future. What was so close is now moving away. One who was your best friend must now act like a stranger or even an adversary. How can this be? Why does this have to be? And how long must you waste.

Get ready for the good part: Your relationship's end gives you an opportunity to create the best time of your life; to learn but not linger, to heal but not hate.

In truth, you can't mourn the loss of someone who's still living. That's a bizarre paradox. Yet, traditionally, we've often been advised to do exactly that. Why then should we be astonished to find that the process of pursuing such an unreal goal is never complete?

Hurt may linger long enough to color and contaminate all your ongoing efforts to relate to other people. Watch out; your motives may be based on the desire to return to the comfort of the familiar. To the same easy, habitual ways that defined you, identified you, completed you. Or so you thought.

The need to restore the familiar may create the expectation that a new relationship will be better just because it's new. We'll just make a few adjustments, and everything will be just fine. But what happens when the new experiences don't click, and we can't achieve the comfort that we seem to remember we once had?

For most people, perhaps you, that can mean running into the same dilemma all over again. Are you prepared to once again give up a piece of your heart? Keep it up, and ultimately, you'll have nothing left to offer a new prospect but guarded mistrust. In essence, that new prospective lover will remain forever on trial for the many mistakes you made with your previous lovers.

Once you have made a genuine recovery, your new life and any new relationships you may undertake will be so much better not because they are new but because of the wiser and simpler path of remembering that because you're human, you already know how to love.

Can you become a virgin again? Perhaps not. But your ability to open yourself to a loving innocence can be recovered. Time, healing actions, and the right kind of insights will make all the difference.

So, on this first day, whether you're relieved or dejected, there is loss to be reckoned with. We urge you: don't do the work, at least the work others urge you to do. You don't have the time, and it will only make you feel less capable than you really are.

Say goodbye to that work myth just like you're saying goodbye to your ex, and instead, let the insights and tips in this book help you to cut through the advice jungle. Let us help you uncomplicate the process. Our method will help embrace a new vision and freedom over the next thirty days—a freedom to love and be loved in the ways you always wanted.[1]

After reading chapter 1, day 1, I was curious how the rest of the book would help me move on with my life. One thing I knew for sure was that I had no interest in looking for love for quite some time. When I lost the *love of my life,* a part of me died too. I searched for anything that would put me on the road to recovery. So many people tried to give me advice, however, none had walked in my shoes.

After Tony's death, I was shocked, heartbroken, angry, and confused. I felt guilty for being the one who was still alive. I questioned myself so many times, asking, *If Tony was suffering with depression and disappointment, why didn't he talk with me? If we had a heart-to-heart conversation seeking a solution to his problems, I am certain together we would have come up with a better solution than suicide.*

One thing that I learned from reading *How to Heal a Broken Heart in 30 Days* was that I no longer blamed myself for Tony's actions and his decision to die by suicide. I learned that it is better to discuss rather than hold my feelings inside. I learned that I am the only person who can make myself feel whole again. But just as I had learned before, I acknowledged that it would take much time to heal.

Once again, I surrendered my life to God. I realized that I am human, and God has control of my life. I admitted that I do not have all the answers and prayed that God did.

Soon after I surrendered, I received a flower arrangement from a friend that contained a stone inscribed "Let Go and Let God."

I smiled. Once again, God had created a miracle through an ordinary person. All I could do was say, "Thank You, God!"

We must be willing to let go of the life we have planned
to accept the life that is waiting for us.
—Joseph Campbell

CHAPTER 11

THE BOOK THAT GAVE ME HOPE

There is truth deep down inside of you that has been waiting for you to discover it,
and that is this: You deserve all good things life has to offer.
—Rhonda Byrne, ***The Secret***

One day I received a phone call from my friend Sandy. As we chatted, she asked, "Have you heard about the book called *The Secret* by Rhonda Byrne?"

"No," I said.

"I'm reading it now. I know you're having challenges thinking about your uncertain future. Try reading this book. I'm confident that once you apply its teaching, your outlook on life will change."

I did not have the vision to see my life in any capacity other than the life I was living. The only positive that I had confidence in was my decision to become a Catholic. And the most reliable positive in my life was my family. They understood my pain and were always present whenever I needed them.

But I trusted my friend and figured, *What could it hurt?* So I bought the book. Before I started reading it, though, I discovered that the author, and the teachers featured in her book, were going to be on *The Oprah Winfrey Show*.

I watched to find out more. Rhonda Byrne explained that in 2004, during a difficult period in her life, she read *The Science of Getting Rich* by Wallace Wattles, which he had written in 1910. That's when she discovered the law of attraction, or what she calls the secret.

The premise is that once you discover the secret, you can start creating the life you want.

Could that possibly be true? I thought as I listened. It sounded as though all I had to do was hold a genie lamp in my hands, make a wish, and wait for the universe to create miracles.

Then I thought, *Hold on, not so fast. For me to create the life I want, I have to* know *what I want!*

For years I lived like I was a mafia wife and did not know it. Tony was the name of the genie who fulfilled my dreams. I put all of my eggs in one basket, and then my basket shattered. I felt empty and confused.

But I promised to keep an open mind as I listened to Oprah's interview with Rhonda. I learned that to become whole again, I needed to let go of my past entirely and focus only on the present's positives. The more I listened, the more fascinated I had to admit I was becoming.

As soon as the program ended, I picked up the book and began reading it. Even though I was excited by the possibilities, I promised myself I would not put pressure on myself to decide about my future.

My friend Sandy was correct. *The Secret*'s teaching inspired me to change my outlook. As soon as I finished reading, I purchased a notebook to record my thoughts and digest the lessons I was learning.

Then I started at the first page and read the book all over again.

The Law of Attraction intrigued me the most. It can be broken down into seven laws. Here's what I realized about each:

(1) The Law of Manifestation

When we think something, we can actually make it become a reality. I recognized that my negative thoughts diminished my positive thoughts. Only when I commit to keeping my thoughts healthy and positive can my circumstances change for the better.

To better put this into practice, I set up a vision board and cut out photos of the things I desired to have in my new life. Every day when I look at it, it helps to keep my dreams alive

(2) The Law of Magnetism

The basic law of magnetism simply states that attraction is everywhere. Whether it's consciously or unconsciously, we attract things and people into our lives by thinking about what we want. The people we attract into our lives is determined by who we are. I thought it would be fun to put this law to the test. Whenever I went shopping, I always found it challenging to find a parking spot close to the store. One day while shopping, I put this law to work. "I need a parking spot up close to open up," I said, sending out my request. Almost immediately, I looked into the next row and saw the rear lights go on and a car begin to back up. By the time I got around to that spot, the car was just pulling away. *This is so simple! I wish I'd known about this law sooner*

(3) The Law of Unwavering Desire

This law means that we are guided by our pure intentions. We are letting the universe know that without a doubt, we are asking for exactly what we want. This law was the most fun. I relied on my unwavering desire and combined it with my requests to God. When I made each request, I thanked God ahead of time for what I wanted. Rather than hope on a wing and a prayer, I asked God with the expectation of receiving. I asked God to bring something into my life that I could be passionate about. God answered by telling me in a letter that I should write a book. I found that request strange because I never had any ambition to do so. I am glad that I listened to God when He spoke to me

(4) The Law of Delicate Balance
The Law of Delicate Balance states to let no fear hold you back. Sometimes I found myself overwhelmed with wanting too much too fast. Previously, I would become desperate and anxious about wanting something before God's timing. Looking back, I discovered that if God gave me what I wanted when I asked, I might not have been open to receiving to the magnitude of God's gift. I prayed for wisdom, and God gave me problems to solve and lessons to learn. I prayed for peace, and God gave me a restless heart to listen. I prayed for love, and God gave me troubled people to help. I learned to trust God in all ways and not put a timetable on my dreams. I learned instead to enjoy myself and appreciate the things presently in my life instead of always looking for more.

(5) The Law of Harmony
This universal law means that we accept others just as we accept ourselves. It is best described with music. The blending of musical notes can create a perfect harmony. Alone, they are just single notes. We are one of the billions of energy forces globally, and we are connected to all energy sources, even if we don't see it or feel it. Everything in our universe is connected and is in harmony with one another. The trick is not to try and dance to the beat of a different drum.

(6) The Law of Right Action
This law is simply to treat others as we wish to be treated. Or what Jesus called the Golden Rule (Matthew 7:12). We need always to be doing the right thing, even when we don't feel like it. The Bible teaches us that God intends our faith and our actions to go hand in hand. My favorite

Bible verse that shows the Law of Right Action is Romans 12:2: "Do not be conformed to this world, but be transformed by the renewal of your mind, that by testing you may discern what is the will of God, what is good and acceptable and perfect" (ESV)

(7) The Law of Universal Influence

This law reminds us that all life is an exchange of energy and that we are all connected. What we do affects others. The energy we emit affects and influences those around us. I discovered that the power of our minds controls our energy. One of my favorite things to do is compliment someone when they least expect it. A simple gesture of saying what I observe about a person makes their day. That simple gesture made one person feel good, and they in turn will compliment others.

After I read through the book, I determined to read it again more slowly so I could continue to process what I was learning. Each night I made a list of the things I wanted to complete the next day. Making a list at night cleared my head so I could get a good night's sleep.

The Secret points out that our thoughts, feelings, and actions have to go in the same direction simultaneously. So the first thing on my to-do list was "Get up." As crazy as it sounded, I felt terrific accomplishing that one task.

The book also indicated that I needed to make decisions based on where I wanted to go, not where I was at the present moment. By living that way, I could release myself from being a victim and begin to take control of my life's destiny. I remembered back to Oprah's show in which she interviewed Rhonda, along with a panel of *The Secret* teachers. One of them, Michael Bernard Blackwith, said, "Nothing new can come into your life unless you open yourself up to being grateful for what you already have."

That was all part of my releasing how I had viewed myself for too long—that of being a victim. The word *victim* plagued my mind continuously. Although many, if not all, people viewed me as a victim, I knew that I had to change my way of thinking to improve my lifestyle and be happier. I felt confident that once I believed in my heart and presented myself as a survivor and not a victim, my world would open up to new possibilities without limitations.

It won't be easy, I thought, but then I whispered to myself, "Take baby steps, just like Mackenzie."

As I had done before, I mentally stepped back from my life to view my circumstances without judgment or emotion (something I realized I would need to do numerous times as I progress through my healing). Before writing notes in my *Secret* journal, I felt the need to rid myself of my constant negative thinking.

I wrote what I needed to do in my new way of thinking.

- Stop blaming others.
- Be compassionate.
- Stop self-sabotaging.
- Perform acts of kindness to others.
- Practice gratitude.
- Work on building my self-confidence.
- Forgive and let go of the betrayals and disappointments.

The last one I double starred to remind me of its importance.

As I read the book and thought back to Oprah's show, I found myself resonating more with the messages the teacher Lisa Nichols offered. She said, "If you were at a restaurant and you placed an order for something, you fully expect it served the way that you ordered it. That's how the universe works. We are putting out orders, consciously and unconsciously."

So the energy that I put out into the world comes back to me, I thought and wrote it down so I would remember it.

I also wrote several of Lisa's quotes:

"If you say, 'I will never have a great relationship,' you won't."

"If you say, 'One day I will meet the love of my life,' you will."

"If you say, 'I will always be fat,' you will always be fat."

"If you say, 'I am working on becoming fit and healthy,' you will."

One of the testimonials I was most impressed with on Oprah's show was from Suzanne Whang. Someone introduced her to *The Secret*, and she was so impressed by it that she spent $3,000, ordering a hundred copies to give away to her friends and family. One of the people she sent the book to was Oprah, thinking, *Oprah must know about this book. She will design a show around* The Secret, *and she will tell the world.*

Suzanne sent a copy of the book to Oprah with a note, but never heard back. A month-and-a-half later, Suzanne heard that Oprah scheduled a show with Rhonda Byrne and the teachers from her book. She found out the date and booked a flight from her home in California to Chicago, where Oprah filmed her show. She also booked a room at the Omni Hotel, where Oprah's guests stayed.

Even though Suzanne was a celebrity in her own right, she still had many desires to live a better life than the one she had the opportunity to create. The significant part about the Law of Attraction is that it is available to everyone, but we must believe in ourselves and God and continuously remind ourselves that there are no limitations in God's world.

Though Suzanne desperately wanted to meet Oprah, she did not have a clue how to make that happen. So she created a Magical Creation Box—using the same principle as a vision board—and put Oprah pictures in her magic box.

Suzanne knew that her thoughts had amazing power, so she began to think about what she needed to do to make her dream come true and open her eyes to the possibilities.

She was delighted when on the morning of her flight, Suzanne received a phone call from Oprah's producer, who acknowledged her letter and invited her to the show. And when she checked into the hotel, she checked in directly behind two *Secret* teachers—Lisa Nichols and Jack Canfield.

She introduced herself and explained some of her story. Lisa and Jack were so impressed that they invited Suzanne to join them for dinner with the other teachers. When they arrived, they discovered that the table setting was for ten. The reservation was for nine people. That extra seat was Suzanne's!

As Oprah said, responding to Suzanne's story, "Doing the best at this moment puts you in the best place for the next moment."

Listening to Suzanne's story gave me patience and faith in the process.

I was so excited by what I was learning through the law of attraction that I wanted to share my newfound wisdom. I bought copies and gave them as gifts. But I was surprised that not everyone was as enthusiastic about my endeavors.

The Secret teachers said it was imperative not to share my dreams with anyone unless they would support me. I found the comment strange until I experienced negative comments from people close to me. Some people accused me of dreaming too big and criticized me for thinking that I could make a difference in other peoples' lives. I was stunned.

One day after hearing yet another negative comment, a thought crossed my mind: *In God's silent words, He promised me wings to fly. And I am going to hold Him to His promise.*

I smiled. *Yes! That is exactly the truth.* I determined that I would remember that thought and repeat it whenever I felt low or whenever someone tried to discourage my choices.

I will succeed at what I want to do—no matter what happens.

One day I was getting dressed for work, and I could not decide whether to wear my Pandora necklace or my strand of pearls. That's when the thought hit me. *Why not create a jewelry clasp that would combine the two necklaces?* I could make a distinctive necklace that would change the face of fashion and capitalize on the $1 billion Murano glass bead industry.

Because I sold jewelry, I knew this was a great idea. I immediately contacted my bench jeweler and worked side-by-side with him for more than one year to create the perfect clasp. I filed a patent and had patents pending, then I made a jewelry line and called it "Kenzie Mac Beth," named after my granddaughter, Mackenzie.

It felt good to take back my life again and to feel the creative juices flowing once more.

The necklace design is a strand of pearls with the catch worn in the front. The jewelry clasp I designed has a locking mechanism. It is designed to fit one Murano glass bead. The cool part is the wearer can change the bead each day to accent her outfit. One day, she can accent with a blue bead, and the next with a red bead.

The possibilities are endless! I thought and smiled. Truth—not just about the jewelry, but about life.

I designed my clasp to fit Murano glass beads from Pandora, Trollbeads, Chamilia, OHM, and more. I wanted to test drive my new invention, so I visited many jewelry stores. All were excited about my creation and immediately set up jewelry shows in their stores. One owner said, "This is the most creative piece of jewelry I've seen in years. My last customer bought two pearl necklaces and six Murano glass beads. That was my largest jewelry sale." Every show I booked, I sold out of merchandise.

I know God would not have planted the seed in my heart if He did not want me to fulfill my dreams. I have learned to always believe in the power of our dreams and never give up on them. But we must be patient since dreams come true in God's timing, not ours.[2]

I truly believe that God has a bigger plan for me and my invention. To this day, more than fifteen years later, no one has created anything similar. The design is very technical. Some manufacturers have attempted to duplicate my clasp without success.

When my husband first died, I couldn't see a future for myself. But God, in His kindness and faithfulness, knew that I still had dreams and purpose. As I allowed myself to heal, I began seeing those dreams and purposes take shape—like with the jewelry.

I look forward to all women wearing strands of pearls with or without a Murano glass bead!

In early 2006 I started to rely on letters from God to encourage me. I did not often request letters from God, even though I knew that God was always by my side. But why wouldn't He speak to me? That's part of prayer. Seeing written letters gave me tangible hope and reminds me that God knows me better than I know myself.

In mid-January, while sitting in church with my journal, I began to write what I was hearing from God.

January 13, 2006

Dear Janet,

Know that it is okay to be hopeful, happy, sad, confused, disappointed, and heartbroken at the same time. Know that every emotion you experience, I also feel. Know that you are never alone, and I am always with you.

Know that you cannot grow without pain. Know that the responsibility of saving others is not yours, but mine. Know in your heart and live through your faith that I only want the best for you.

You have demonstrated over and over again that your heart is pure. You have shown that you are a good person and are dedicated entirely to me. Your actions and continued dedication do not go unnoticed.

I have grand plans for you. . . .

For months, you have been praying for the truth, knowing that the truth would set you free. As so many people say, "Be careful what you pray (ask) for."

I am glad to say that you know that prayer works. You have greater strength and wisdom than many others do. Now it is your turn to live your best life. Do not look back.

Love,

God

I received other letters from God throughout the year. Including one special letter that came after I was struggling with some physical pain. I was fascinated with a jewelry client who had a black belt in karate. She was a little older than me, and physically she was in great shape for her age. She told me that her life changed for the better physically and mentally when she introduced karate into her life. I was desperate to add physical activity to my daily routine and to break up the monotony of sitting behind a computer for hours each day.

I signed up for karate classes and looked forward to my first lesson. When I entered the class, I discovered I was the only adult! The children and adult schedule had changed, and the instructor did not notify me. My instructor insisted that I stay. Even though I felt out of place, I enjoyed watching the children and did my best to keep up with their routine.

At one point during the class, the instructor said, "Now we are going to run around the room, jump on the small trampoline with one leg, and karate kick with the other."

Though my mind told me that I could perform the task, my body said, "Absolutely not!" My body went to the left, I lost my balance, and I crushed my right knee. I lay on the floor crying as I waited for help. A friend came and drove me to the hospital. As it turned out, I tore the ligaments in my knee. That was the end of my karate career.

September 15, 2006

Dear Janet,

I know you feel like your heart, your body, and your spirits are broken. Know that your heart should never feel broken. Know that I (your Father) love you so very much. Your body is hurting right now, almost to the point of tears. Know that you have taken steps, with My guidance, to lead you to the proper people who will help take away your pain.

Now, let's address your broken spirit. My question to you is: "Why do you feel that your spirit is broken?" Just as you heard many people say, including yourself, "When nothing is happening, God is working."

The past five years have not been easy for you. It seems like no matter how hard I make your test, you have passed it. Maybe not the first time, and that's okay. You have learned much with each disappointment.

Know that I have chosen you to do an exceptional task for Me. Know that you could not perform this task unless you knew in your heart that when the time arrived, your confidence would be grand to succeed.

You cannot say to someone who is hurting that you feel their pain unless you have walked in their shoes. . . .

Never be afraid to share your story. It will encourage others to have faith. Believe in yourself and know that I am always by your side.

Keep the faith (your faith) always.

Love,

God

I continued to write in my journals and requested God to write back to me. At the time of my request, I felt that my pain over everything I had experienced was pretty much in control. And yet, on

January 12, 2007, I received this letter from God about pain when I least expected it.

Dear Janet,

Pain. So many people wonder how such a small word can have such a complicated meaning.

There are so many different types of pain—from hurting a finger to losing a loved one.

There is the pain of suffering, and there is the pain of disappointment.

There is the pain in not knowing, and there is the pain in knowing too much.

There is the pain in having your heart broken, and there is the pain in your heart, wondering if you will ever be loved again.

There is pain that you feel for others, and there is pain knowing that you cannot take someone else's pain away.

There is the pain when you think of My Son, who died on the cross, and there is the pain of sadness, knowing that only a small percentage of people have come to know Me, as you are getting to know Me.

There is the pain and disappointment in your own heart, knowing that it took almost fifty years to acknowledge Me and My incredible powers.

There is a touch of fear with pain in wondering and hoping that you will live for a long time so that you can discover more about Me and your feelings.

You want to share your feelings with so many other people so they can become the best that they can be and share My Word with others.

Fear not. With every pain, you experience growth. With every pain, you become closer to Me and gain a better understanding.

Fear not. I am holding you in the palm of My hands, and I will never let you fall.

Love,

God

In 2008, the Great Recession hit the USA, which caused large numbers of unemployment and people to lose their retirements and savings. The bottom fell out of the luxury jewelry industry, and I did not have the money to support my jewelry clasp project. Each week I visited my jeweler in Philadelphia to have customer repairs done. But that wasn't enough money to sustain me.

My jeweler's wife, Silva, worked for Apple Vacations. One day while I was picking up some jewelry repairs, Silva was visiting her husband at work. We got to talking about the state of the economy and how it affected my business and livelihood.

"Why don't you sell vacation packages?" she suggested.

I wasn't sure how I could make money selling vacations in the middle of a recession. "Are people even traveling right now?"

"You'd be surprised," she said. "People need to escape for a while. I think you'd be really good at it. Even doing it part-time could bring in a little extra money for you."

I needed the money, that was true. But I also needed to have a little adventure in my life. "Okay, I'm willing to give it a try!"

I worked twenty hours a week for seven months making $10.60 an hour. I wasn't going to get rich, but I thoroughly enjoyed it. And I discovered I was good at it. In seven months, I sold more than $850,000 in vacation packages. Corporate asked me if I would be interested in opening a travel agency to sell their products. That was quite a compliment. The company had never asked anyone the same request in fifty years.

I agreed and used the office that I had subleased in my condo building to sell diamonds, fine jewelry, and now all-inclusive travel vacations. I obtained a travel license and formed a new company named Golden

Luxury Travel. I poured my attention into building the business and making it succeed. Even though the jewelry business was down, the travel business seemed to hold its own. Again, God was taking care of me.

I loved owning a travel agency. I got to travel at discounted rates and have fun. Occasionally, I had the opportunity to book a group of people with the same interests. My favorite booking was for a golfer's group to Secrets Resort and Spa in Puerto Vallarta, Mexico. I hosted the trip and played golf. Everyone had a wonderful time!

Between opening a travel agency and designing a jewelry clasp, I seemed to be living out *The Secret*'s law of attraction. I continued to study the book and write down my thoughts. In fact, the author suggested the readers write things down. I searched Amazon to see if Rhonda Byrne or any other teachers offered a journal to write in, and they did not.

I had a brilliant idea! I reached out to Rhonda Byrne through her publicist, John Stellar. "Is Rhonda creating a journal as a companion to her book, *The Secret*?"

He responded quickly. "No. Presently Rhonda is working with a team to have *The Secret* translated to Spanish, French, and other languages. Writing a companion journal is not in her plans."

When I told John about my idea of creating a journal to complement *The Secret*, he said, "That is a great idea. Let me know when you complete your book, and we will talk."

For the next six months, I worked day and night to create a journal worthy of being a companion to *The Secret*. I envisioned my name in lights right next to Rhonda Byrne's. That visual kept my dream alive. My new project gave me hope for a better future.

After completing my book, I again contacted John to let him know I was ready to move forward with Rhonda.

"I am sorry, Janet, but we cannot partner with you," he told me. "I forgot about our No Partnership Policy that the corporation put into place." Rhonda Byrne's attorney sent me a certified letter stating that I could not use her name, any of the teachers' comments, or any quotations from *The Secret* in my journal companion.

Though I was disappointed, I didn't feel it was a total loss. The theory behind *The Secret* is that we are in one stage of our lives and desire to be in a better place. No matter how many obstacles get in our way, we must *stop*, pick ourselves up, and focus on the end goal.

I started rewriting the journal and titled it, *My Secret Journal*. My life and dream did not skip a beat. I purchased the domain name: www. mysecretjournal.com. It's fantastic how purchasing a domain name for $10.95 allows you to dream BIG.

It took me another six months to rewrite the book. I set up each page so the writer could write directly to God. Each page had quotations and positive affirmations. I self-published it on April 10, 2008—my husband's birthday.

I met with a marketing specialist, Rick DeDonato, to help me promote the journal. "Your book is good, but it's not great," he told me. "Most self-help books are written by people who have a doctorate. Why would someone read your book when other people are more qualified to write?"

His question took me to a place where I did not want to go. I remember biting the inside of my cheek. Just the thought of reliving my terrifying moments made my body feel weak as my heart began to race. I started to cry.

I explained how Tony had died and that I wasn't certain whether it was suicide or murder. And I shared about the shocking secrets I discovered afterward and how it put me in a deep state of despair. "My life after my husband's death put me in a fetal position. But then I became a Catholic. As I grew in my faith, I started writing letters to God. One day, I asked God to write a letter back to me. He did. And today I am in a much better place."

When I finished telling my story, I looked at Rick. His face showed a mixture of surprise, sadness, compassion, and bewilderment. And tears slid down his cheek.

"Your story is amazing. You need to rewrite your book to include it. People will gain strength reading about the adversities you faced, how you stood up to your challenges, and how you recovered. I hope you aren't too upset with my comments?"

"No." I recognized that his request and my acceptance was the first time in twelve years (since I opened my jewelry business) that someone had challenged me to rise higher.

I realized that I had to raise my level of thinking, find Janet, and give more of myself. In truth, I did not know where I was going or how I was going to get there.

I appreciated that he viewed me as a survivor seeking victory, not as a victim. He saw what I had hoped for—and said that when people heard my courageous story of hope and survival, they would find ways to bring hope into their lives.

"If you could survive what had happened to you, then others can find hope and survival too," Rick said. He thought they would view their life circumstances differently and look for out-of-the-box thinking to change their lives. "People will become more credible witnesses for them to help others as well."

I left that meeting and went home to follow through on his suggestions. And though I had good intentions, I found that I was not emotionally prepared for the assigned task. Even though years had passed since Tony's death, unbeknownst to me, the scars of his death, betrayal, and a multitude of disappointments were like fresh stab wounds to my heart.

I thought I was healed. I thought I was over this. Will this pain ever go away?

With mixed emotions, I renewed my commitment, though, to rise to the new challenge. But I realized that's life. We move forward, we get drawn back, but we continue to keep our eyes ahead. And even when we don't think we have anything to share to help others, we can know that God has chosen us to make a difference in others' lives.

Through His letters to me, God began to help me truly understand that our survival story will bring hope to others when we go through a tragedy. So we need to wear our battle scars proudly as badges of honor and survival. They become part of our healing and give a new purpose to our lives.

One day I ran across the poem "Be Thankful." It spoke to me and gave me many things to think about.

Be Thankful

Be thankful that you don't already have everything you desire.
If you did, what would there be to look forward to?
Be thankful when you don't know something,
for it gives you the opportunity to learn.
Be thankful for the difficult times.
During those times, you grow.
Be thankful for your limitations,
Because they give you opportunities for improvement.
Be thankful for each new challenge
because it will build your strength and character.
Be thankful for your mistakes.
They will teach you valuable lessons.
Be thankful when you're tired and weary
because it means you've made a difference.
It's easy to be thankful for the good things.
A life of rich fulfillment comes to those
who are also thankful for the setbacks.
Gratitude can turn a negative into a positive."
—Author Unknown

I worked hard at viewing my life through a lens of gratitude. I continued faithfully attending church. I was putting much effort into working *The Secret* principles into my life. But even though I focused my attention on the positives, nothing seemed to be happening. Every day seemed to be the same as before.

I decided to enjoy the journey and not worry about the destination. I am discovering that God has a bigger plan, more generous than I could ever imagine. And I could finally say, if asked, I would not change anything that had happened in my life.

Find a way to be thankful for your troubles, and they can become your blessings.
—Unknown

CHAPTER 12

HOW TO REMAIN POSITIVE IN A CYNICAL WORLD

The weak dread the storm, the foolish invite the storm, the wise avoid the storm,
the strong battle the storm, and the great overcome the storm.
—Matshona Dhilwayo

I was alone and had been for many years. Business was almost non-existent. The recession of 2008 dropped me to my knees. The money in my savings accounts assisted me in the down markets, but they didn't cover everything completely. I seemed to live in a constant state of anxiety and stress, though I never told anyone or asked for help, because I did not know how I would pay them back. But also because I was embarrassed.

It seemed every day I heard about a jewelry store filing for bankruptcy. Jewelers were selling gold for scrap and placing diamonds and fine jewelry in pawn shops to generate enough cash to pay their employees. Fortunately (and unfortunately), I was not alone. We were all victims of life's circumstances.

I robbed the proverbial Peter to pay Paul and robbed Paul to pay Peter. Peter broke his leg and Paul fell down the stairs. And still the business and personal expenses continued. My credit cards were at an all-time high. My mortgage and car payments were two months behind.

The stress of making less than minimum payments on credit cards overwhelmed me. I had entered into agreements with good intentions and planned to pay off the credit cards before the introductory rates expired. The introductory rates were excellent; however, a late payment allowed the banks to raise the interest rates to 27.99 percent on some cards.

Many years prior, a friend suggested that I obtain a private banker's assistance within my bank. For any banking needs, I merely sent one email or made one phone call. We talked at least twice a week. I was grateful for the ease of banking and their attention to detail. As I sat in the middle of a recession, the bank went out of its way to restructure my mortgage to make my payments more manageable during these troubling times. They did what their policies would allow, however, the "deals" did not last long.

Several months later, the combination lock on the two-thousand-pound safe in my office broke. Inside, locked securely, was my entire inventory. I needed it to sell and make money, but I delayed calling a locksmith because I did not have an extra $1,000 to pay to have the locked drilled and the combination reset.

It was the beginning of the month again, and payments were due. A friend suggested that I take the jewelry I owned to an upscale pawn-shop in exchange for cash, until I could get back on my feet and get my inventory back. But that meant calling a locksmith. Although I felt degraded by the process, I refused to turn to family or friends for assistance. I had created the problem, and I needed to deal with it on my own.

I knew my jewelry would be secure at the pawnshop. The government controls the interest on the money that pawnshops charge. The interest charged is 3 percent per month or 30 percent for a year. Six months of interest paid on time would allow the jewelry to stay in the pawnshop safe until I could satisfy the loan's original amount.

Though I did my best to pay off the loan, I was not able to pay for all of it. That meant, I could forfeit the jewelry and the pawnshop could sell it and keep the profit.

I dreaded making a phone call to my jeweler to admit the problem, but he immediately paid the balance. He paid $5,000 for my jewelry, valued at $20,000 wholesale. Though I was embarrassed, I was grateful that he stepped in. I made the offer to my jeweler so they could make extra money. I did not request to repay to get my jewelry back.

Since I became a person of faith, I discovered that God always showed me how to fulfill my needs. I uncovered avenues that I never knew existed, and miracles happened when I least expected them.

One time I made a $4,600 error in my checking account. At the time, I balanced my checkbook every three months. Before balancing my account this time, I made a diamond sale for $4,600 to the penny. I accidentally entered the deposit twice. When I found the error (after entering my new transaction), I sat back in amazement. *How cool was that? God had my back, even when I did not know that my back needed covered.*

I truly believe that God lets us struggle, but He will not allow us to fall. There are times when we need to be humbled, and there are times when God shows us that we truly need to depend on Him for everything.

I knew in my heart that God would help me without asking; however, I also knew I could acknowledge God's miracles more with my eyes wide open. I continually surrendered my life to God, especially when I was uncertain of the next step to take. Whenever I felt like I was losing my faith, I reviewed past miracles that God had performed in my life.

I knew I needed Him now. Being alone, without any support, weighed on me and started to affect my confidence. Especially when I compared myself to my daughter. She was successful in her career and fitness. She held the title of the fastest woman marathon runner for the state of Delaware for many years. She was a constant achiever, while I felt like a failure. While I was proud of her accomplishments, I wondered why God was allowing me to continue to drift.

But it was through my daughter that God provided rescue. My 401k was one-third of its original value, and my savings account was much lower than I wanted it to be. I was a financial embarrassment to myself and knew I would be to my daughter, if she knew. I am sure that she did know. One day she called and invited me to live with her and Mackenzie (Amy was now divorced).

I agreed, though I hated to leave our condo and my memories.

After I moved in with her, she witnessed me struggle to find my strength and confidence. She responded by challenging me with tough love. During my more difficult days, I thought about suicide occasionally. My life appeared destroyed after my husband's death, family and friends walking away from me, attorney issues, financial issues, and now I was on the verge of declaring bankruptcy. Since I knew firsthand the pain and suffering that Tony's death put me through, I was not about to do the same to my daughter, granddaughter, family, and friends.

Even with that decision, it didn't lessen my pain as I continued to wrestle with my confidence and lack of faith every day. Depression and anxiety attacks got in the way of moving forward. I was waiting for God to help me, but I think God was waiting for me to do my part.

Where is God? I wondered. *And why did He put dreams in my heart of making a difference in other peoples' lives, if I can't even get my own life together?*

And so once again, I committed to starting over. I returned to opening God's teachings into my life. I turned again to Joyce Meyer, Joel Osteen, T. D. Jakes, and *The Hour of Power* presented by Dr. Sheila and

Dr. Robert Schuller. Their messages always seemed to give me strength as I listened and digested their words. God was using them to fill and empower me.

One speaker on the *Hour of Power* was Bishop Kenneth Ulmer. He delivered a message titled "The Lord of the Storm." His message seemed directed toward me and the challenges I was facing.

Bishop Ulmer asked his listeners to define their storm, customize it, and identify with the storm's message. He explained that in the Bible, a storm is *not* just a storm. A storm begins in the water, moves over the mountains, passes the valley, and ends in the desert. It is always moving.

According to Bishop Ulmer, everyone is in one of three places: We have just left a storm; we are in the midst of a storm; or we are headed toward a storm.

If we aren't in a storm, often we have no clue that one is coming. Even if we just left a storm, we may have another one headed our way.

But instead of being afraid, we must look to our Lord, who sits as King above the storm. No matter our storm, God reigns over it. It is not too big or powerful for Him to handle. God is there before, during, and after the storm. Through faith, we can seek God during a storm and run to Him for shelter. He will protect and help us endure.

Listening to this message encouraged me to meditate on God's promises and remain strong, knowing that all things through Christ strengthens us. So I thought about two verses in particular:

The LORD will fight for you; you need only to be still.
(Exodus 14:14)

Have I not commanded you? Be strong and courageous. Do not be afraid; do not be discouraged, for the Lord your God will be with you wherever you go.
(Joshua 1:9)

Less than one week after receiving God's message from Bishop Ulmer, I found myself experiencing a natural disaster rainstorm. It lasted for more than two hours and was the most treacherous storm I had ever witnessed. Eighty-mile-an-hour winds caused extensive damage to the greater Wilmington area.

Television newscasters interviewed children, who spoke of the horror and said they feared for their lives. They watched trees uprooted and roofs torn from their houses. A tornado ripped a house in half, only miles from my home.

No one can control the power of a storm. And yet without warning, the rain stopped, the wind calmed to a cool summer breeze, and the storm disappeared. The sun shone brightly, and the color of the grass and flowers shone brilliantly. It was as if I had just exited a scene from a movie.

Although the surrounding area did not escape the storm's terror, the view from my window appeared as though it had never happened. There was not one drop of water on the ground to show that a storm had passed through my neighborhood.

Later that night, I thought back to the weather report that Bishop Ulmer predicted: "After every storm, the sun always shines." The wickedness of that storm symbolized the turbulence I was experiencing in my life. God provided the dominant visual to restore my faith and give me hope and courage to face my fears. It gave me the strength to get through another day and look forward to every next day.

Before I heard Bishop Ulmer's message and experienced that storm's actual occurrence, I didn't realize the *true* power of hope. Before, it had been just a four-letter word.

The day after the storm, I woke up remembering a dream I had experienced a few weeks prior. The setting was a large hotel overlooking the ocean. I was in a room with many women who appeared to be in good spirits. However, I noticed one woman lying on the floor, gasping for air. I checked her throat to see if she had anything blocking her air passage, then I repositioned her to help her breathe better.

Without warning, a murky pond of mud appeared beneath her head. Soon part of her hair and face were submerged. Almost immediately, she uprighted herself as though nothing had happened. Later I saw her leave the restroom all cleaned up with two blue bows in her hair.

The last part of the dream was in a terrible storm. The lady with the two blue bows appeared and introduced me to her brother. I didn't stick around to see if he was a matchmaking connection.

As the storm intensified, I noticed children in trouble outside in a nearby parking lot. Without thinking, I ran out to assist them. When I left the building, though, I found myself in a twister of a storm, like the tornado in the *Wizard of Oz*.

It lifted me and the others around me, and we began to fly. But instead of being scared, we were all in control.

Dreams can be crazy! I thought when I awoke. *What's the symbolism of the blue bows?*

I decided to take a closer look at the color blue and found that it is often associated with depth and stability. It symbolizes trust, loyalty, wisdom, confidence, intelligence, faith, truth, and heaven.

Bishop Ulmer said that God is above the storm. It is our choice to listen or not to listen to the voice of God. We can choose to do things on our own, with strife and frustration, or choose to obey God, accept His grace, and perform our tasks with ease.

If we question our faith, I believe we feel weary and have no energy to move forward. I think it is because we expect things to happen quicker than God has chosen for our timing.

Being a person of faith, I have learned that when I run to God for His love, help, and security, He provides comfort and takes away my fears. I have learned that embracing God and God's grace is the only answer to every question.

I had so many storms in my life that I called upon Monsignor Lemon for guidance. I viewed him as my closest ally to God. On every visit, he would ask, "What does your heart tell you to do?" On one visit, I remember complaining about God and questioned His existence.

"Why would you walk away from the only One who can save you?" he asked. "Why would you walk away from the only One who will never leave or forsake you? Why would you walk away from the only One who can give you absolute hope during a storm? Why would you walk away from the only One who can provide you with unconditional love and accept you just as you are?"

His questions seemed more like an inquisition.

"Janet, we only grow in our most challenging times. What does your heart tell you to do?"

I did not recognize or digest God's message to me through Monsignor Lemon until the next morning. I knew that if I stayed in bed, kept my bedroom door closed to the outside world, and turned off my phone, I would have a peace-filled day. No stress, no worries, and no thought of ignoring the unpaid bills sitting on the kitchen counter. I also knew that something dramatic had to change in my life, or I would find myself in the same disappointing position for years to come.

I began to ponder Monsignor Lemon's words and then consider the dream God had given me in which everyone flying and in control.

What am I in control of in my life that I started but did not finish?

The answer was clear. I wrote *My Secret Journal* and self-published it. I took it to a marketing agent, and he said that I needed to rewrite my book to include my story. That was it!

I needed to finish that project.

I got out of bed, got dressed, and felt in control for the first time in a long time as I sat down at my computer and began rewriting the book to include my story. It took me a while, but after several months, I completed and retitled it, *My Victory Journal.*

It was done, but now what? I was still in control. I couldn't just write the book, I needed to move forward with it. So I did some research and contracted with Steve Harrison, cofounder of Bradley Communications in Philadelphia, to publish and promote my book. I joined their Quantum Leap program to work with coaches. Even though I was in control, I knew I was not qualified to perform the task on my own; I needed to work with professionals.

My first coaching call was with Barb Early. I gave her a synopsis of my book.

"Why did you write the book?" she asked.

"I self-published the book *My Secret Journal* and presented it to a marketing agent. He requested that I rewrite the journal to include *my story*."

"No," she said. "Why did you write the book?"

I wasn't sure what she was going for, since obviously I wasn't answering to her satisfaction. "I want to help others get to know God, the way that I am getting to know Him."

"*Janet*," she said loudly, obviously to get my attention. "Why did you write this book?"

"I want people to know that there is life after suicide."

"That's the title of your book."

"What book?"

"The book you are going to write."

I was confused. "What about *My Victory Journal*?"

"It will be published one day. But you must write this book first."

I thought about it for a moment. "I created a quote that has brought me a lot of hope and encouragement. Do you think it should be part of the book?" Then I told her the quote, "In God's silent words, He promised me wings to fly. Come hell or high water; I am going to hold Him to his promise."

"That's your title—*There Is Life After Suicide: God Promised Me Wings to Fly.*"

I got off the phone excited about the possibilities.

The next day, I received a call from my second coach, Mishael Patton, and brought her up to speed on what I'd discussed with the first coach.

"We will change the title of your book," she said after listening intently. I was confused again! "What are we changing it to?"

God Promised Me Wings to Fly: There Is Life After Suicide."

I hung up the phone, filled the bathtub with hot water, and soaked in the tub for hours crying. I was disheartened by the call and the new request. I felt relieved when I finished writing *My Victory Journal* and looked forward to the next step of preparing for a beautiful life. Now with one phone call, I felt overwhelmed with the amount of work she was suggesting. As I sat in the tub, I prayed for guidance. Immediately, I felt a calming peace enter my body and I stopped crying.

My coaches had asked me to go to a place where I had never been before. One thing I knew for sure was that my coaches saw more in me and my story than I saw in myself. Once again, I was told to write my story to share with others. I reminded myself of the words my marketing coach said many years earlier: "Your story will help others to find strength after a tragedy and you will help others gain a better understanding of themselves with renewed hope."

I did not have a clue where to begin. I knew in my heart that God was directing my steps, but this fork in the road was one I could never have imagined. I thought I was just supposed to write and publish the journal. But this . . . this was entirely different.

I did nothing for several days except pray for God's guidance. I had written in journals after my husband's death, but I hadn't read them. But as I prayed, I felt God leading me to pull out those journals and read them to help me understand better the man I was married to, the traumas I faced, and the courage I managed to muster up to move on with my life.

I knew that many people face traumas and challenges and wonder how to endure and move on with their lives. I had been one for so many years. For every step I had taken forward, it seemed like I was taking two steps backward, constantly trying to move on and heal. Some days I succeeded; others not so much. But perhaps that was the point. Perhaps if I wrote my story with all its struggles, that would be just the thing to help others experience hope and find a new purpose for their lives.

I can do this, I thought, remembering the idea of being in control. No one else could write my story. And if this was how God was truly leading me, then I knew I needed to listen and obey.

I created a vision board and cut out pictures of a healthy woman, diamonds in the rough and cut diamonds. Many years before, God had given me a dream of living in a yellow house in Florida, so I also posted a photo of a yellow house over which I stamped "Paid in Full."

I thought more in-depth about the idea of diamonds in the rough. When I was fifteen years old, I started working part-time in the jewelry industry. By eighteen, I managed the store. At the age of thirty-one, I had worked for two department stores supervising twenty-five fine jewelry departments. Though I loved the experience, I needed to change my life or I knew I would spend the next twenty years in the same position. So I quit and opened my own business as a fine jewelry and diamond broker, which I operated for twenty-three years. Now I had worked in the jewelry industry for more than thirty-five years and felt burned out. The past five years had been a constant struggle financially, and I needed something new to look forward to each day.

I became discontented living in Delaware. It was time to move. I hoped that I would find my happiness in Florida. I had visited the state enough to know I enjoyed it. Plus my sister Diane lived there, so I wouldn't be completely alone. Even though I knew that the grass was not always greener on the other side, I was willing to take that chance.

My life started as a diamond in the rough. Looking back on it, I could see how my characteristics were much the same as the definition for diamonds in the rough:

> Someone (or something) that has hidden exceptional characteristics and future potential, but currently lacks the final touches that would make them (or it) truly stand out from the crowd.

The phrase is metaphorical and relates to the fact that naturally occurring diamonds are quite ordinary at first glance, and that their true beauty as jewels is only recognized through the cutting and polishing process.[3]

As I moved forward with my written plan and deadline dates, I reminded myself that diamonds show their best under pressure. Surrendering my life to God was the first and best of my decisions.

I knew in my heart that if I was determined to be my best, I needed to handle the worst. Polishing diamonds to perfection requires friction. I knew that God would not make me go through so much pain without having something extraordinary on the other side.

Working through trials and tribulations would put me on the road to satisfaction and inner peace.

One day I was sitting in my church's chapel, I searched for something to read from the literature provided. The one thing I was still struggling with was my disappointment of not seeing progress promptly for the efforts I put into place.

I picked up a poem by Naomi Long Madgett and read it slowly. God amazed me one more time with His faithfulness:

Woman with Flower

I wouldn't coax the plant if I were you.
Such watchful nurturing may do it harm.
Let the soil rest from so much digging.
And wait until it's dry before you water it.

The leaf's inclined to find its own direction.
Give it a chance to seek the sunlight for itself.
Much growth is stunted by too careful prodding, too eager tenderness.
The things we love we have to learn to leave alone.[4]

God's message to me was clear—through the storm, the dream, the diamonds in the rough, and now the flowering plant poem—that He is ultimately in control. That He can use my pain, even the suicide and its aftermath, for His glory. That He longs to heal me and strengthen me. That He has given me dreams and a purpose that are not cancelled because of what I experienced. That even when I stumble and fall, trying to get my footing, He is still beside me, picking me up and setting me back on the path. Not once, but over and over and over—as many times as I need Him to.

> *God turns coal into diamonds with time and pressure.*
> *He may be doing the same with you.*
> —Unknown

CHAPTER 13

FINDING FORTUNE IN THE MOST UNEXPECTED PLACES

Success is the good fortune that comes from aspiration,
desperation, perspiration and inspiration.
—Evan Esar

I n January 2010, while at Mass, I heard Monsignor Lemon share a story about a devastation one of our church families had experienced. On January 5, at around 9:30 p.m., the Riveras found themselves in the midst of a massive house fire, in which they had only minutes to get to safety. Their next-door neighbor's house had caught fire, and the flames had jumped over to the Riveras's home, quickly engulfing it. They ran out their front door with the clothes on their backs. They could not even save one photo, let alone clothes, furniture, or other treasured items.

"Felix Rivera has been in charge of our maintenance department for more than twenty years," Monsignor Lemon said at the end of his sermon. "Their insurance only covered the shell of their home and very little of the interior. I would like for us to take up a collection for Felix and his family. They need money, clothing, furniture, or anything you can donate to help them rebuild their lives and home."

Although I had been a parishioner at Immaculate Heart of Mary Church (IHM) for nearly twenty years, I had never heard of Felix. But my heart still went out to him and his family. Tragedy is tragedy. But $20 was the best I could do—especially as I was about to lose my home too.

It still felt surreal even to think about it. All my hard work over so many decades. All the pain I'd gone through with my husband's decision to end his life. And now this. Sometimes when yet another storm came, I wondered, *How much more of this can I take?*

Besides completing the requested paperwork for my attorney, I did little preparation to end one colossal chapter in my life. It was just too much to face, so each day I kept myself occupied with busy work, hoping that would make the fear and anxiety attacks disappear.

The luxury jewelry business was the first to go in a down economy, and most likely, it would be the last to recover. During the good years, I would sell five or six diamond engagement rings a week. But by 2010, I was lucky if I sold one ring each week. I thought I was holding my own, but day by day, I slipped further behind.

But I kept trudging on, hoping that somehow a miracle would appear to help me right myself financially.

It didn't, and by November, I received a notice that the state had scheduled a sheriff's sale for February 10, 2011. I had three months to vacate my property and find another place to live.

How can I sort through decades of my life and of my life with Tony in just three months—and find another place to live? "God, You have to help me!" I cried out.

God heard and answered. My daughter, Amy, invited me to live with her and Mackenzie until I could find a permanent place to live. With gratitude, I accepted her offer.

And then slowly I got to work, sorting, throwing out, piling to give away, and then boxing up those things I would keep.

As I continued to work, I remembered the Rivera family and wondered how they were managing, now eleven months later. I stopped by the rectory not long after that to inquire about them. The secretary gave me his phone number, so I called and introduced myself.

I explained to him that I was moving out of my house to live with my daughter and that I had furniture and accessories I would like to give his family, if they still needed items.

"We have nothing. We would be grateful for anything," he said.

They have nothing after eleven months? How can that be? Our church had taken up an offering.

As if reading my mind, he said, "We are so grateful for the money the church provided to allow us to rebuild our house. So we haven't taken any items other than money right now because we've had no place to store them. But the target date for the house completion is the last week of December, so your timing is perfect. I will give you a call when we are close to moving in."

By January I was still waiting for a call. My anxiety was growing, because now the sheriff's sale was less than one month away. I called Felix. "I'm under a deadline to remove everything from my home. Can we set up an appointment for you and your wife to view the items?"

He agreed, and we set a time for his wife, Maria, and him to visit in a few days.

Before their arrival, I labeled items to give away. Boxes and larger items labeled with "Felix" written boldly with a black marker were in every room. Some items I had tagged, but then removed the labels when I changed my mind—only to rethink the decision and relabel the same boxes and items again. It was challenging to part with many possessions. Some of the pictures I gave away were part of a joint decorating venture with my husband. I donated them with mixed emotions.

Felix and Maria arrived right on schedule. They seemed like a lovely middle-aged couple.

I walked with them from room to room and pointed out the items labeled with the orange notes filled with Felix's name.

"Are you giving us all of the labeled items?" Maria asked, her voice holding a hint of awe.

"Yes. I will be moving the balance of the furniture to my daughter's home, and the smaller items I will be putting in storage."

Maria fell in love with many of the things and oohed and aahed over them. She commented that one pedestal and accessory would look nice next to their picture of The Last Supper. She was going to place a statue of the Blessed Mother on the pedestal.

I was pleased to hear their plans.

My gift included three wall units, a black marble dining room table, television, washer and dryer, chairs, pictures, linens, bedspreads, draperies, garbage disposal, as well as many other items. Before their arrival, I reviewed all the items in my kitchen and placed the things that I would give away on the kitchen counter, including a twelve-piece place setting of dishes, one frying pan, and kitchen utensils.

Maria cried when she saw the dinnerware. "We have been eating off of paper plates," she said, as she wiped at a tear. "Are you giving us the frying pan too?"

"Yes," I said and smiled.

Maria clapped her hands with joy.

"Why are you so happy with a frying pan?"

"Since the fire, we have only had one pot to cook food."

Without hesitation, I pulled out all of my pots and pans and gave them to her.

Her eyes grew wide and filled with tears. "Are you sure?"

"Absolutely."

She insisted that I keep at least one pan for myself, since I was not vacating the property for thirty days.

Within one hour, Maria and Felix packed ten large plastic tubs with dishes, pots and pans, accessories, and linens.

"Enjoy the dishes. I never even used the coffee cups and saucers," I told them.

"We drink our coffee in coffee mugs," Felix said.

"I have many mugs in storage. I will get them for you when I have a chance to go through the items in my storage bins."

The following weekend, Amy and my sister Billie came to help clean out my storage silos.

"Where do you think you're going to live once you find a place?" Billie asked.

"Florida."

She and Amy both stopped their work. "Florida?" they asked in unison.

I smiled. "Yes. When I was eight years old, I had a dream that I lived in a yellow house in Florida. I'd say it's about time I see that dream realized."

They uttered their surprise but could see that my mind was made up.

As we sifted through my belongings, I kept very little and gave or threw away the rest. Because I kept my office in the building where I lived, the building manager allowed me to rent storage space since I would be losing my space I had that went with the condo.

When I packed the new silos with my stuff, my belongings seemed to have more meaning. I sparingly chose the items that I wanted to keep. I reminded myself of my dream that one day I would live in a yellow house in Florida. With that dream in mind, I kept only the items I could visualize in my new home.

It is interesting how our minds work. Here I was at a turning point, with no money, and I was thinking about my dream house in Florida.

While cleaning out the storage, I found coffee mugs and placed them aside for Felix. After my daughter and sister left, I began to wrap them individually in newspaper. Tony and I called the coffee mugs our "love mugs."

Each morning we would drink our coffee from a mug hand-selected by the other. If Tony left for work before I awoke, he would always leave a "mug love" message.

Sometimes he had several mugs stacked in a pyramid to show how much he loved me. He was consistent with the small actions of showing his love to me. That was one of the reasons why I never questioned his love and loyalty.

After he died, I put them in storage because my heart broke every time I looked at them.

Now I wrapped each mug with care. I picked up a white mug that had "Tony" written in red across it. Next to it was another mug with a raised Tony the Tiger cereal figure etched on it.

I began to wrap them for Felix and Maria's collection, when I paused. *How stupid is this? The mugs had special meaning for Tony and me. No reason to include them with these others.*

I stopped wrapping them and set them aside, out of my view.

Felix arrived a few days later with his son to move some of the larger pieces of furniture. "My family is very grateful for your gifts. I would like you to meet my son, Tony. He is strong, and he will be helping me today."

Though I heard Felix introduced his son, we engaged in a conversation right away, so I couldn't remember exactly what he'd said. "I'm sorry, Felix. What is your son's name?"

"Anthony. We call him Tony."

My jaw dropped. *Those mugs . . .*

"Tony, I have a special gift for you."

He appeared puzzled, especially since I did not even know he existed until a few minutes before.

I began searching for the mugs but could not find them. It appeared that I had buried the sight of my memory deeper than I expected.

As Felix and Tony began to break down a wall unit, I continued searching, until I located them behind some boxes in the living room.

"Ah!" I declared loudly and walked with the presents, holding them up excitedly. But as I began to present my "special gift" to Tony, I stopped suddenly. My heart fell into my stomach and I began to cry. I stood in the middle of my living room, shaking with fear—the fear of losing mixing with the fear of holding on.

Felix and Tony looked on, unsure how they should respond, so they stood uncomfortably until I could regain my composure. "My apologies. It's just that these are special to me."

I held the mugs momentarily as a mother would grasp onto a dying child. Even with all the secrets I'd discovered about my husband, I still cherished the moments of what we'd had. Now it was time to let go.

"My husband's name was Tony," I said and explained about the love messages we created for each other using the mugs.

I began to cry again, feeling myself on the verge of an anxiety attack, when Felix kindly and compassionately put his arms around me. Tony joined in for a group hug—something I desperately needed at that moment.

Our Lord works in mysterious ways. I had been helping out the Riveras, and they were now helping me. *I certainly didn't see that one coming.*

"Do you have a queen-size bed?" I asked, as I placed a custom queen-sized bedspread with matching custom draperies into a box for them.

"No. I wish we did, because the bed we are sleeping in is tiny for two adults."

Several weeks later, while talking to my friend Sandy, she asked what seemed like a random question. "Do you know of anyone who can use a queen-size mattress and box spring? I'm moving out of my three-bedroom house to a two-bedroom apartment and need to get rid of some things."

My yes came quickly! When I told Sandy about Felix and his family, she enlarged her gift. Not only did she give Felix and Maria a queen-size mattress and box spring, she also gave them a bed, headboard, two dressers, two nightstands, a mirror, and two lamps.

Our Lord certainly creates miracles through ordinary people. What an amazing God!

In exchange for my gifts, Felix, Maria, and their two sons surprised me with a gift. They moved my remaining furniture into my daughter's house. They also removed all of the custom closets from my condominium, installed them into Amy's house, and took the rest for their home. What started as a goodwill gesture turned into something even more beautiful.

They even helped me gift appliances to my next-door neighbor Dorine, whom I adored. She was a fantastic cook and used her kitchen appliances so much that her stove had a lot of wear and tear. Her dishwasher was on its last leg. At eighty-five years old, though, Dorine was hesitant to buy new appliances. So Felix and his sons removed the two more modern appliances from my home and installed them in Dorine's kitchen.

Since the appliances and closet hardware was all paid for and I owned them outright, I didn't give it a thought about donating them to other people. We put Dorine's old appliances in place of my newer ones. I figured a new owner would gut the condo anyway, and make it into the home of their dreams.

As I walked through the condo for the last time, now bare, I had mixed feelings. This had been Tony's and my home. Leaving it meant leaving behind so many memories, and I felt sad. But it was time to move on, to get on with living. I could still take the memories with me and hold the good ones close to my heart. And that gave me a sense of anticipation for my future.

My foreclosure did not make me bitter. I did the best that I could under the circumstances. After my husband's death, my financial situation was still fine. In hindsight, though, I should have paid off the mortgage. I never dreamed that the economy would take a dive into the toilet and take me along.

And yet, I felt that this foreclosure was God giving me another chance to move forward with my life. I would never have taken that giant step on my own. Truthfully, I was too afraid. I was living a comfortable life—it was a boring life, but it was comfortable.

Every day I rode the elevator down six floors to go to work, and every night I rode the elevator back home. The only time I left my building was to pick up my granddaughter at school or go to Philadelphia for business. Talk about mundane!

But the events that followed my need to vacate my home turned my life from mundane to surprising adventure and blessing. And really, it started when I decided to bless others with what I had been blessed with. It seemed like the more I gave away, the more the phone rang. New business started knocking at my door. I had often heard that God wants to give us so much more than we have, but we need to rid our lives of the things we are not using to make room for that more.

After a while, business slowed down, but that was okay. I needed the downtime to rewrite my book and get my head together.

I moved into my daughter's home with my granddaughter, my daughter's fiancée, and his golden retriever named Tucker. While I was grateful for my daughter's hospitality, I was also aware that I was invading her family's privacy, so I spent 95 percent of my time in my bedroom. I ate there, I worked there, I relaxed there. I knew for sure that I needed to find Janet and figure out a way to save money to move out on my own.

But spending so much time alone wasn't healthy. Even though I claimed it was to honor my daughter's privacy, the truth was that it kept me from having to face the reality of where I now was in life. The more disconnected I became, the more I felt myself falling back into the trap of insecurity, in which my strength and confidence began to drain away.

And my daughter was seeing it too.

"We need to talk," she said one day, after knocking on my door and stepping inside. "I'm concerned for you. This isn't healthy for you to stay in this room so much. It's time for you to come out and start living. I'll help you."

Those weren't empty words. She was like a drill sergeant showing me tough love. Many times, her tough love was so intense I felt like running away. I knew she was doing this from her heart, but it was not an easy road for either of us. Tempers grew short and words flew that sometimes were better left unsaid. But she was right. I needed to get out.

I needed to keep my faith healthy by attending church. I needed to work at consistently making myself a better version of me. And I couldn't do those things locked up in a bedroom.

I joined a gym and religiously worked out three times a week. I decided that I needed to revisit the items I had placed in my storage silos and reduce them in preparation for my move to Florida. *Perhaps I can sell some to make some money*, I thought, knowing that I had much to do to build my bank account before I could ever think about moving.

My church was having a rummage sale to raise money and asked parishioners to bring items they wished to sell. The church would then split the proceeds with the sellers.

I ticketed and offered more than seven hundred items, from furniture to kitchen utensils. At the end of the event, I netted $800. What I didn't sell, I either returned to storage or donated to Goodwill.

Reflecting on my giving, I recognized that God was giving me more than I gave away. Curiosity got the best of me about what the Bible said about giving, so I looked up giving on an online Bible site. I discovered that while *love* is mentioned 714 times in the Bible, *giving* is mentioned 2,172 times. *Giving is really important to God*, I realized.

I learned that firsthand back in 2009.

In March of that year, I went to Philadelphia to meet with diamond suppliers. I parked in the same lot where I always parked and passed by the homeless people perched on the street corners. Philadelphia has a Jewelers' Row district, which is the oldest diamond district in America, dating back to 1851. Many people visit and stroll down the historic brick-paved Sansom Street that is in that area. Since South Philly is known for having a homeless population and almost no services to help them, homeless people gather in that area and ask for help where visitors are spending money.

Every day, I passed a legless man in a wheelchair, who sat on one corner, and a young girl who sat on the ground on the opposite corner. In one hand she held a handwritten message on a dirty piece of cardboard that read, "Please help me. I am homeless and hungry." In the other hand she gripped a worn paper cup, holding it out to passersby so they could drop money in.

Most of the time, I donated to their cause, hoping that my cash would buy them a decent meal. Other times, I walked by, because I was in too much of a hurry. And sometimes, after I walked by, I would hear a voice in my head telling me to go back and put something into their cups, which I did. I always tried to follow what God requested me to do.

At the end of one day, I walked steadfastly to my car and passed the young girl sitting on the sidewalk. The temperature was about twenty-five degrees. While talking on my phone, I gave little attention to what appeared to be a dirty, bad-smelling human curled up in a fetal position. At first sight, it looked as if she was merely trying to keep warm.

This walkabout was different from the other times I'd passed by. Out of the corner of my eye, I noticed that she was crying. As she wept, she clutched a pamphlet from a nearby Catholic church. It was so cold it appeared that the demons of winter could have taken her life at any moment. I told my caller, without explanation, that I had to hang up immediately.

I returned to the young girl and stooped to her level. "What is your name? And why are you crying?"

"My name is Tara. I'm crying because a man called me ugly and said I was a worthless human being."

I was surprised that such a comment would hurt a homeless person. *Why should she care about the comment if she chooses not to get herself off the street?*

The thought then surprised me. *Wait a minute, Janet. Who are you to judge someone when you don't know the circumstances behind her situation?* Maybe she did care. Perhaps she had tried to better herself and failed, or maybe she felt she was beyond hope and gave up.

"I suffer from an autoimmune disease. I have difficulty walking due to the winter's cold and I do not have money for medication."

I felt like crying, but held my tears inside. "Why are you not living in a homeless shelter?"

"I need to have an identification card to get into the shelter," she said.

I was naïve to a situation such as this. That's one of the blessed downfalls of being a devout Christian, knowing what we know. We are always keeping our eyes open for hurting people, especially those crying out for help, regardless of our consequences. We are always seeking to help hurting people—emotionally, physically, spiritually, or mentally.

"How much money do you need to get an ID and get into a homeless shelter?"

"I can request the necessary paperwork by mail, but it could take four to six weeks to receive, or I can take a bus to my birthplace in northern New Jersey to obtain the ID the same day."

I gave Tara money for the bus, the documents, and a few meals. I also gave her my cell phone number and asked her to keep me posted on her progress and call me if she needed help. I felt giving her a chance to start a new life would give her hope.

As I walked away, I heard a voice in my head say, *Give her your gloves.*

What? You want me to give her my gloves, too?

I returned to Tara's side and did as God commanded.

After a few days and some complications resolved, Tara gave me a call. "Thank you for helping me," she said. "I took the bus to New Jersey, got my ID, and found a place to live in a project home outside of Philadelphia. I need to meet with people from the Outreach program to complete the paperwork, and they will drive me to the project home."

A man named Christopher Miller called me and identified himself as the owner of the house. He thanked me for my willingness to help Tara and applauded me for my efforts.

The room cost $50 per week plus a $5 fee for a key deposit.

"I need to charge a deposit for the key because people are always losing their keys," he explained. "I am also changing my organization's name and will be changing banks. So for the time being, it would be best if you pay in cash due to the change's timing."

I met with Tara the following day on Broad Street in Philadelphia. I gave her a ride to the convention center, where she would meet the Outreach representatives, and I gave her $200 for a month's rent, plus $5 for the key deposit, and $100 for spending money. In turn, Tara gave me the address where she would be living.

When I returned home, I gathered three large suitcases filled with clothes, sheets, towels, bath products, robe, slippers, and even feminine products. I was not leaving any wants for a homeless person to start a renewed life. Goodwill deeds of clothing and more filled my SUV.

I called Tara to find out how things were going at the convention center.

"I'm scheduled to meet the Outreach representatives at 3:00 p.m. and should arrive at the house by 5:00 p.m."

"I will meet you at your new home to help you get settled," I told her.

When I arrived in the neighborhood and searched for the home, I became very uncomfortable. And the thought of getting out of my car terrified me!

Before knocking on the door, I called my friend Gloria and gave her the house address. "If I do not call you back after thirty minutes, please call my daughter and call 911."

I rang the doorbell and knocked on the door, but no one answered. Just as I was leaving, an older, toothless, disheveled-looking woman came to the door.

"Is this the Outreach project home?"

"No," she answered.

Very confused, I attempted to call Tara and Chris without success. I left an angry voice message for each.

I got back in my car, feeling that I'd been scammed. *How did I get myself involved with two very deceptive people?* I called Gloria to assure her that I was okay. I felt I could never tell my daughter. She would accuse me of being gullible and naive.

The next morning, I received a phone call from Chris. "I'm sorry I was not available when you called yesterday. The Outreach representatives kept Tara busy with paperwork, and she did not arrive until 8:00 p.m. The woman you spoke to at the house is part of the Outreach program. They are not permitted to tell others that they are in the program."

I sighed with relief. "Thank you for your explanation."

Two days later, Tara called me. "Thank you for all you are doing for me. It felt terrific to take a shower and sleep in a bed. It's much better than sleeping under I-95. Chris took me grocery shopping, and I am making new friends."

This is excellent news, I thought, feeling terrible for my distrustful way of thinking.

I called Tara back. "I would like to deliver items of clothing to you tomorrow."

"No one will be at the house tomorrow," she said. "We need to vacate the house because an exterminator is coming to spray. Chris is taking everyone to Philadelphia for lunch and sightseeing."

"Oh, well, I want to make sure you get some things."

"I'll have Chris call you. He can give you more details."

True to her word, as soon as we hung up, Chris called me. He confirmed that they would be in Philadelphia the next day and not at the house because exterminators would be spraying for roaches. "By the way, Tara is making great progress. I am very proud of her. The older women in the home are treating her like she is their daughter."

This would work out better for me, since Philadelphia was twenty miles closer than the Outreach home in northeast Philadelphia. "Where can I meet you?"

Chris gave me an address in Center City, Philadelphia, where we could meet and scheduled our meeting for 3:00 p.m. the next day.

An hour before we were set to meet, at 2:00 p.m., Chris called. "Hi, Janet. I need to reschedule. I just received a phone call from another Outreach home. They have a crisis that needs my immediate attention. I will call you tomorrow morning to set up a time and place to meet."

But at 9:00 a.m. the next morning, Chris called and again cancelled. "Where is Tara?"

"Tara is in Philadelphia."

Knowing that Tara had to take several buses or a train to go downtown, I became suspicious. So I called Tara. "I just spoke with Chris. He said that you're in Philadelphia. What are you doing there?"

"I'm at the Philadelphia Art Museum."

Finally, I came to my senses. I did not buy that one!

"Tara, if you set one foot on the sidewalk for even one minute, the whole deal is off." I felt outraged.

"I sat on the Sansom Street corner this morning because I didn't have any money."

I had been duped. "Either you are going to get off the street or not. You cannot have it both ways. I'm done!"

I never called Tara or Chris again.

Losing the money out of stupidity was one thing. I knew that all of my goodwill deeds would not go unnoticed by God and felt in my heart that He would reward me one day for my caring and generosity.

God teaches us many lessons—especially those learned in disappointments. Looking back, I viewed the circumstances as God's way of alerting me to something bigger that would be coming my way. I prayed that it would be a reward for my efforts. But I also realized I had been so gullible the first time, I knew I needed to investigate future opportunities that might come my way.

A few days later, I received a phone call from a potential client who found me through my diamond website. I received a selection of diamonds to show. He drove two hours to meet with me. It was my first loose diamond sale from my website. His total purchase was $10,000.

"Thank You, God. I am very grateful."

Two weeks after the experience with Tara and Chris, I was heading once again to my diamond supplier. There Tara sat on her reserved sidewalk seat where we'd first met. My first thought was to walk by and mentally kick dirt in her face. Soon I felt a calming voice within me, like clouds opening up after a storm, urging me to stop.

I removed my sunglasses and stooped to her level to talk with her eye to eye. "How are you doing?"

"Not well. Someone stole my bag with my cell phone. I wanted to call you, but I couldn't.

The temperature was below freezing, and I noticed her hands were bare. "Where are the gloves I gave you?"

"They were in the bag with my cell phone."

Now it was my turn to talk. When I began, I wasn't sure what I was going to say. Even though I knew that my words would fall on deaf ears, and Tara and Chris were professional scammers, I felt the need to express my feelings.

"Tara, you and Chris are very good at what you do. Sadly, you have lowered yourself to begging on the streets and scamming people. You have no dignity and no self-respect. God sees everything you do. As much as I want to report you to the police, I am walking away. God will be the vindicator."

Before she could say anything, I walked away and never looked back.

In August 2009, six months after my encounter with Tara, I talked with two women who worked at a jewelry store in Philadelphia. They told me that they saw Tara and her boyfriend, Chris, cleaned up and experiencing the "Best of Philadelphia" events on the weekends. To my knowledge, Tara and Chris are still working the streets of Philadelphia.

God sees our hearts and rewards us for our actions. He gives us wisdom, guidance, love, and miracles through ordinary people. We aren't responsible for the other person; we are simply responsible for our own actions. I acted in good faith; God will honor that. He is 100 percent there for us. I have learned to trust God for His timing, believe in Him, and always walk in faith. I take action on the things I feel good about and dream of a fantastic future. I depend on God to do the things that I cannot do.

God chooses all of us to make a difference by helping others. Random acts of kindness can make a tremendous impact on a person's life and make a difference in our lives too. God's timing is always perfect.

Shortly after that last interaction with Tara, I received a phone call from a commodity company in Philadelphia that specialized in many things except diamonds (according to the representative who called me.) "The company owner has a friend who owns a diamond mine in Columbia. We want to capitalize on an opportunity, but we know nothing about the diamond industry and where to sell diamonds. Would you be interested in taking a look at the inventory and consider being our broker?"

Knowing that most diamonds come from South Africa, Russia, Australia, and Canada, I listened to his presentation with caution and curiosity. He emailed a copy of the prospective company's diamond inventory, categorized by shape, color, clarity, and carat weight. The company sought to bring fifty thousand diamonds into the United States with a wholesale value of $40 million. Although skeptical, I continued to listen.

The second phone call included the name of the company supplying the diamonds. I researched the company and found out that they were part of a family that sold noncertified clarity-enhanced diamonds.

It appeared that the company was planning to bring fifty thousand clarity-enhanced, fracture-filled, noncertified, and bogus-certified diamonds into the country. Unsuspecting clients (mostly internet buyers) would purchase the diamonds to save money, thinking they were getting a diamond at a bargain price. Then once a diamond was sold, and the customer found out it was not the diamond represented, they could not return it. The company would claim that the client switched the diamond.

I spoke with representatives from the Jewelers Mutual Insurance Company and the Jewelers Security Alliance Committee. Both felt they targeted me to be part of a horrible fraud and con game.

Thank You, God, for opening my eyes to take a more in-depth look into a business opportunity that could have ruined my life. It pleased me to know that God was watching out for me—as He does for all of us—and teaching me lessons along the way.

It also helped me to continue writing in a journal to God and having God write back.

On what would have been our twenty-second wedding anniversary, I decided to visit my husband's grave. We got married on April 22, 1988. This was the first time in five years since I had visited his grave. I was surprised by so many feelings that came rushing back to me. I brought my journal with me so that I could write a letter to God while I was there. But instead of receiving a letter from God, I received a letter—from Tony. I was surprised by God's intervention.

Dear Janet,

I feel the pain that you hold in your heart, because I am the reason for your pain. If I only had a better understanding of how love should have been shared rather than the way that I squandered it around . . .

Look at you. Twenty-two years ago today, we got married. I died almost nine years ago, and yet here you are acknowledging me on this day.

My first question would be, why? Why have you not moved forward—at least looking for love? You want love, yet you are afraid to put yourself out there to find it.

Believe me. My words are real. I love you very much, but I want you to move on. I was a fool—a fool to think that I was invincible; a fool not to recognize the true love we had for each other and build upon it, rather than seek outside ways for sexual pleasure.

I have said many times. It was just a game, and it was a game that I lost in the end. I destroyed my life. I ruined the lives of many others with my selfish, immature ways. I thought I was rich and powerful. The reality was put in place as I sat with a gun in my hand, not prepared but feeling forced to end my life.

The pain of my life's consequences was too massive to bear. I certainly did not feel rich and powerful; I felt inadequate and pathetic. I was weak. I was sad. I felt so alone and felt the thought of losing you and shaming my family would have been more than the pain and suffering that I would have had to endure.

My death was inevitable. I am sorry. Sorry for more than you will ever know. However, one thing that I am not sorry for is meeting and falling in love with you. I will always love you, but now you must release your heart from me to find a new love.

Love,

Tony

Not long after, I asked God to speak to my heart. And I received a letter from Him as well. These were nothing I created on my own. I simply allowed my hand to transcribe what I heard.

Dear Janet,

I hope you feel better. Your broken heart is a natural feeling. You wonder if your heart will ever be happy again, and love will burst from the seams.

Trust My words. Your heart will love again. Now your heart is not open to receive. Life is hard right now, and you question My existence more often than you think you should. You believe in Me (as well you should). You are thankful at the end of the day for getting through each day.

You get involved with many projects and have great ideas. You keep occupied with busywork. Do not get discouraged. It is not busywork. You are accomplishing things one baby step at a time.

Remember your sister Diane's words. "Take baby steps, just like Mackenzie."

Right now, your house is a mess. It is a reflection of how you feel internally. Overwhelmed, cluttered, two steps behind, frustrated with lack of rewards for your efforts, bewildered, directionless. It seems like every direction you choose, you put much hope in the project seeking financial freedom.

You feel unaccomplished. Please do not give up. Plant more seeds and sow your seeds. Create a plan and write your goals with deadline dates. Be consistent with your progress. I know you are confused and seek direction and guidance. Your cry for help does not go unnoticed.

Write down your concerns and depend on Me to do the things that you cannot do. You must do your part, and I will do the rest. Plan your day by scheduling exercise, work, meals, and phone calls. Stick to a plan and work your plan. Be regimented, and all things will work together for good.

Love,

God

That time at Tony's grave, along with those two letters, gave me the strength to stop defining myself as a widow. I am not a victim. I am victorious!

Later that night, once again I opened my Bible randomly. It seems that when I do this act, God always leads me to the perfect passage to satisfy my questions and enrich my soul. He did not disappoint:

Instead of your shame, you will receive a double portion, and instead of disgrace you will rejoice in your inheritance. And so you will inherit a double portion in your land, and everlasting joy will be yours.
(Isaiah 61:7)

Give, and it will be given to you. A good measure, pressed down, shaken together and running over, will be poured into your lap. For with the measure you use, it will be measured to you.
(Luke 6:38)

In addition to the messages I received in my letters, I thirsted for more wisdom and encouragement. The more I read the Bible, the more I became fascinated with God's Word. In the Old Testament, God's people were going through a very dark time. I could relate to many of the struggles that people faced thousands of years ago. I was more fascinated with the miracles that God blessed upon His people simply because they remained faithful to Him, even in those dark times.

I discovered through the Old Testament that our days are destined to shine brighter when we do not give up on God. I was living proof that by staying in faith and being obedient to God's Word, I was receiving more than double for my trouble.

My bankruptcy and foreclosure were behind me. I owned nothing except for my car, which became a top priority. In reality, I had nothing to lose and everything to gain. I reignited my dreams with new vigor and determination and made a firm commitment only to look forward and never backward.

I'm looking forward to influencing others in a positive way.
My message is you can do anything if you put your mind to it.
—Justin Bieber

CHAPTER 14

THE SECRET REVISITED— MY SEARCH FOR STRENGTH

God didn't add another day in your life because you needed it,
He added it because someone out there needs you.
—Author Unknown

I n September 2013, I revisited *The Secret* to seek ways to renew my strength and create a better vision for my future, a future different from the one I was living. I needed to go way outside of my comfort zone and think differently. I reminded myself of the dream that I set in place when I was eight years old—that I was going to live in Florida in a yellow house. But here I still was, in Delaware, still living with my daughter and her family.

For eight years, I had declared that I would not endure one more winter in Delaware, but I never put anything in motion to make the change. When I reread The *Secret*, I was struck anew by the story about the author's sister Glenda, who desperately wanted to move from Australia to the United States. Glenda understood the Secret, and was doing everything to make what she wanted happen. But as months passed, she found herself still living in Australia.

"Glenda looked at her actions and realized she was not 'acting as if' she was receiving what she had asked for," wrote Rhonda Byrne, *The Secret*'s author. "So she began to take powerful actions. She organized everything in her life for her departure. She canceled memberships, gave away things that she would not need, and she got her suitcases out and packed them. Within four weeks, Glenda was in the United States working out of our U.S. office."[5]

Glenda's story encouraged me. If one person did it, so could I.

Rhonda Byrne continued with the point, which resonated with me:

> Think about what you have asked for, and make sure that your actions are mirroring what you expect to receive, and that they're not contradicting what you've asked for. Act as if you are receiving it. Do exactly what you would do if you were receiving it today, and take actions in your life to reflect that powerful expectation. Make room to receive your desires, and as you do, you are sending out that powerful signal of expectation.[6]

I made a list of the things I needed to accomplish. This time I put a written timetable in place. I printed six months of calendars—from October through March. On March 31 I wrote, "Day 1." I marked the other days on each calendar block as a countdown for my moving date to Florida. On October 1, 2013, I planned to be living in Florida in 182 days.

When people asked me to commit to something, I graciously refused and told them that I was moving to Florida in ___ days and needed to complete my goal. This time, nothing was going to stand in my way. I set my dream in place with a deadline written in stone (or in this case, ink).

On my list of things to accomplish was a massive undertaking that I had put off for years. Every psychic I spoke to told me that my husband left a letter of explanation with a family member regarding his untimely death. But his family had never apprised me of a note. And since we were no longer on speaking terms, I'd had nowhere to turn for answers.

I remembered that a member of my husband's family spent time in our church's chapel every Sunday evening from 11:00 p.m. to midnight. One Sunday, after leaving my sister's house, where we had a family dinner, and I consumed a lot of wine, I got the courage to meet my in-law face to face. Although he was an usher at our church, I rarely saw him.

I arrived at the chapel at 11:15 p.m. When I entered, two other people were there praying. I quickly spotted Tony's family member sitting near the front. I sat at the back of the chapel for twenty minutes, trying to get the courage to approach him. The effects of the wine had worn off and now my stomach was in knots.

I found a pen and paper and wrote, "What did the note say that Anthony left?" I clutched the note for more than ten minutes and then thought, *It's now or never.*

I slowly walked to the chapel's front and asked permission to sit next to him. Though he was surprised, he granted my request. My knees shook so hard I was afraid we'd be able to hear them. Looking straight ahead, I presented the note to him and waited for his reply.

He quietly read it. I could feel his eyes on me. "What note?"

I explained that I talked with many people and spoke to many psychics. They all insisted that Anthony left a note.

"There was no note. If there was a note, I am not aware of it."

"You are a liar!"

"Do you think I would lie to you in front of the Blessed Sacrament?"

"That's why I am asking you in His presence."

"Look. After Anthony died, our family had accountants review the company's books. They discovered many discrepancies. I decided to leave the company and start a new life." He paused. "I hate Anthony!

Every day I wake up, I think about him and how he destroyed our family business."

I wasn't sure I wanted to believe him.

"Look at me!" he said and waited for me to turn my head. "Every day I look into the mirror and get sick to my stomach."

He did look different, worn out, aged. And yet his face looked exactly like my husband's. I stared into his eyes. He was telling me the truth.

The only thing I could figure was that the accountant for the family business had discovered that Tony embezzled money. This family member had been upset, but I could see that he'd never expected Tony to take his own life.

I slowly stood, pleasing that I had, at least, done what I'd set out to do. As I turned to walk away, I felt compassion for this man sitting before God asking for forgiveness. And I had no doubt that God would grant it.

God sees us when we are in pain. Sometimes He steps in immediately. Other times He allows us to endure the pain to learn a lesson. Sometimes we go around the same mountain over and over again. When we finally decide, *No more*, God steps in to heal us and takes away our pain in His timing.

It was time for me to stop wasting any more time wanting to get revenge on the people who hurt me. The Bible says to let God be the vindicator. I knew that my strength came from God, and once again, I surrendered my life to Him. I knew that God heard me the first time. The repeated action was more for me than for Him.

When I returned home, I pulled out my journal of quotations, flipped it open to a random page, and began to read a quote by Joel Osteen:

God knew there would be unfair situations. That's why He's already arranged a comeback for every setback, vindication for every wrong, a new beginning for every disappointment.

It amazed me that I turned to the exact page and quote to help put closure to my past and give me hope for a better future.

I felt empowered. I had made my peace with my husband's family, and I was putting my plans into place for my move. As I pondered this quote, I remembered something that had happened a couple years before. I decided to visit my sister Diane in Florida. I booked a flight on Frontier Airlines from Philadelphia to Orlando and upgraded my seat to first class for only $100.

When I sat in my assigned seat, I noticed a cell phone lodged between my seat and the window. "Oh no. Someone lost a cell phone."

"That's my phone. I dropped it," said the gentleman sitting next to me.

"If you knew you dropped it, why didn't you pick it up?"

"I left it for you to pick up."

I decided not to talk to this crazy man and prepared to watch *The Secret* on my iPad. I put earbuds into my ears and settled myself.

The man pulled the earbud from my ear. "My name is Francisco Santiago. My friends call me Frankie. What are you watching?"

I was stunned by his forward and unconventional behavior. "I'm watching a show about the book *The Secret*. Have you read it?"

"No. Can I watch it with you?"

"Okay," I said, again surprised. I figured I'd explain some of it before we watched. "*The Secret* is about the Law of Attraction. A friend introduced me to the book, and I'm fascinated with what I am learning. Applying the teaching to our lives has the power to transform us. We simply need to believe that anything is possible."

"That sounds interesting," Frankie said. "Can we share your earbuds?"

We began watching, and throughout the flight, I would occasionally stop the film, so we could engage in an in-depth conversation about the show and ourselves.

I discovered that Frankie took an early retirement from Acme Markets, a grocery store chain located in the northeastern part of the United States. He drove a tractor trailer for them. Previously from Delaware, he moved to Orlando to enjoy retirement and play golf.

Since golf is my passion, I couldn't help but feel as though he was seated next to me for a reason. *I think I just made a new friend.*

We became so engrossed with the movie that we did not notice that the plane had landed and everyone had debarked. We were the only two passengers left on the plane! The flight attendant requested that we gather our belongings and debark. As soon as we got to the waiting area, we sat and watched the movie until the end. We exchanged phone numbers and promised to keep in touch.

Over the next few months, we became the best of friends. We spoke almost every day. Frankie wanted more of me for a relationship, but my heart was not open to receive. He accepted the conditions of our friendship and we fell in love with each other to the point that we were comfortable talking about anything.

I visited Florida often to visit my sister Diane and Frankie. And he visited Delaware frequently.

My family fell in love with Frankie too. My nieces and nephews called him Uncle Frankie.

My relationship with Frankie gave me even more of a reason to push forward with my plans to move to Florida. A couple months before my Day 1 of March 31, 2014, I flew down to Florida to find a rental home and, hopefully, a job. I found a house to rent about twenty minutes from Diane's house, and one hour from Orlando, where Frankie lived.

That was easy! I thought.

Next, I turned my attention to securing a job. As much as I would have liked to semi-retire in Florida, play golf, and write books, my savings account would not sustain me.

I applied at a local jewelry store, not far from my house, and received an interview right away. The owner, Wendy, offered me a full-time position making excellent money. A week after I accepted the job, Wendy called and offered me a position managing her store, increasing my salary by $5,000. It looked like *The Secret* was working.

With the housing and employment handled, I returned to Delaware and immediately went on a FAM trip with Apple Vacations to Puerto Vallarta. A FAM trip is a free, or low cost, trip for travel agents or consultants provided by a travel operator or airline to promote their service. On this trip, twenty travel consultants stayed at two different resorts and visited twenty. The purpose of the trip was to get agents familiar with the resorts to sell more vacation packages.

A few weeks later, I put together a group of women with similar interests, including golf, and revisited Puerto Vallarta. My commission check was more than $2,000. Things were definitely looking up for me.

While on the trip, I received an email from my real estate broker, Marie. "I have bad news for you. The owner of the house will not rent to you because you declared bankruptcy in 2010."

I leaned back against my chair and sighed. *What am I going to do?*

Even though my bankruptcy was three years prior, and I confirmed that I had a new job in place, the owners of the house would not take the risk. I was devastated knowing that I was moving to Florida in less than one month and did not have the time or money to revisit Florida to rent another home.

I viewed hundreds of homes available for rent on Zillow. It was vital for me that I rent a house and not an apartment. During my lifetime, the only house in which I lived was my parents' home, and I left that one in 1970 when I got married. When I married the first time, we lived in several apartments and then bought a townhouse. When I was with Tony, we lived in an apartment and then purchased a two-bedroom condominium in a luxury building.

I found another house to rent with a pond in the backyard. It looked perfect! Although it was a little older home, it had a brand-new kitchen. I received a copy of the leasing agreement and prepared to sign it, when suddenly, I stopped. I asked Diane if she would make an appointment with the realtor to view and take a picture of the backyard.

The house shown on the MLS listing, with a beautiful pond, appeared to be one step above an infected insect pool. Even though my decision to rent a house was time-sensitive, I knew this was not the house to rent.

I revisited houses for rent and found the perfect one. A good thing, as I was moving to Florida in less than ten days. I completed the application and waited to be accepted. The owner refused my offer, because of my bankruptcy. Again, I was devastated. My dream of moving to Florida was disappearing one application at a time.

I decided to write a letter to the homeowner and place my life on the table. I explained that my husband died tragically in 2001; the jewelry business declined in 2007; and I was forced to file for bankruptcy in 2010. I owned a fine jewelry and diamond business for twenty-three years, supervised twenty-five fine jewelry departments in two major department stores, designed a jewelry clasp with patents pending, authored one book, and was in the process of writing another book. I also owned a travel agency and had secured a job managing a jewelry store in Florida.

I laid my heart and soul on the line. I detailed every accomplishment I had ever achieved and presented what I was working on in the future. Once I mailed the letter, I turned my circumstances over to God. I did everything in my power and prayed that God would intervene.

It worked. The owner accepted my application.

I asked Diane to view the home before I signed the contract, and she said it was perfect. It was a three-bedroom home, 2,119 square feet, with two full bathrooms and a water view of a wildlife preserve where many colorful birds visited each day. Even though the house was painted in warm brown earth tones, rather than yellow, I still felt excited about this new step forward in my life.

The house is located in Viera, a suburb of Melbourne, and is only twenty minutes from the ocean. The best part is that Viera, I learned, means *absolute faith and unwavering belief in the Lord.*[7]

I had a massive sigh of relief for a minute or two. I called Frankie with the great news.

He was excited too. "I will fly to Delaware and drive the truck with your belongings to Florida." Then he paused for a moment. "I haven't been feeling well for some time. However, I will not let you down. Count on me."

A few days later, Frankie called. "Hello, Juanita. I am in the hospital."

"What? Frankie, what happened?"

"Yesterday I woke up exhausted and felt weakness in my legs. I was having trouble walking, and I have no strength in my hands. I cannot even hold a cup of coffee."

"I am so sorry for you."

"I don't think I will be able to help you—"

"Don't worry about me. I'll make other arrangements for my move. The most important thing is for you to find out what is causing your symptoms and get well."

Two days before my scheduled move, doctors diagnosed Frankie with ALS (Lou Gehrig's disease). With ALS, your mind stays sharp, but your body becomes so weak that you cannot do anything. Like many ALS patients, the symptoms gradually increase. Because of the way it presents itself, many people diagnosed with it often hope to beat it. Frankie remained optimistic.

True to his word, though, he arrived in Delaware the day before my move. Nephews, my sisters, and many friends helped move my things into the truck, while Frankie directed the process. I also hired a professional mover to assist with maximizing the truck's cabin space. My sisters helped me clean my daughter's home of any sign that I ever lived there. That was important to me. I wanted to honor her and her hospitality by making it as clean and neat as I could.

Though Frankie and I wanted to hit the road as quickly as possible, my sister Billie took one look at Frankie and wouldn't hear of it. "You look exhausted. I think it would be best if you two got a good night's rest and drive tomorrow. I'll make dinner for us."

We agreed and planned to leave around 6:00 a.m. to avoid rush-hour traffic around Washington, DC.

The drive took two days. I don't remember driving from Delaware through the state of Virginia. I was crying so hard that I barely saw the road. I had lived in Delaware for sixty-five years. I was leaving behind my business of twenty-three years, my family, and my friends. I knew the life I desired was not in Delaware, and I was praying that my new life in Florida would be different, better.

I looked for any sign from God to let me know that I was not making a mistake leaving my life behind as I drove 858 miles to my new home. I looked for messages of faith, hope—or of anything!—on every truck that passed and every street sign I viewed. God was not showing me any signs of hope, which made me nervous. I began to question my decision every mile as I got closer to my destination.

When we arrived at my new home, I leaped out of my car and started to cry.

"Why are you crying?" Frankie asked.

How could I explain what I was feeling, when I wasn't even really sure myself? "The house is perfect. Let's go out back to see the water view."

We found many ducks swimming and four-foot Sandhill cranes. It looked like a little slice of heaven. As we watched the calm water with its mesmerizing currents, peace slowly washed over me.

"This is beautiful," Frankie said. "I will visit you often."

We walked to the front of the house to wait for the realtor to join us to let us inside. My next-door neighbor was moving out of their home to downsize after living there for ten years.

I introduced myself. She was pleasant and told me, "It's a beautiful, safe neighborhood. You will enjoy living here."

"Thank you," I said.

"Did you see the cross in the water? The house owner put a four-foot handmade pipe cross in the water for the birds to perch on and dry their feathers."

She led Frankie and me back around to see it. It was just as she said, and a white swan was even floating next to it.

I looked to the sky, raised my hands, and declared to God, "You put a cross in my backyard?" At that moment, I knew that everything was going to be more than just okay.

The scene stayed with me, and later when I got my internet hooked up, I googled to find out the spiritual significance of swans and found one interesting explanation:

> If a swan has glided into your path, she will help show you . . . new ways of thinking, breathing, and going with the flow. She asks that you accept your ability to know what lies ahead. Be sure to pay attention to your feminine intuition, hunches, and gut instincts. Remember your inner grace and inner beauty. Let it shine forth for those around you to see. . . .
>
> Realizing your own true beauty will unfold the ability to bridge new realms and new powers. Some of the spirit swan animal's symbolism is awakening the power of self, spiritual evolution, transformation, peace, tranquility strength, and confidence.[8]

It also said that the swan can indicate an ability to look into the future and accept a constant presence of healing and transformation.

I believed that God placed the swan there to remind me that He is always with me. My new life was beginning with God's blessing.

As I was unpacking boxes and settling in before starting my job, Wendy, the jewelry store owner, called. "Would you be willing to attend a jewelry convention in Scottsdale, Arizona, the week after you start? You'd go with Susan, our graduate gemologist, to buy diamonds and fine jewelry. Also, it will be an excellent way for you and Susan to get to know each other."

I immediately agreed. I had never been to Arizona and was excited about the trip. But I was also eager just to start working in a field I loved and felt confident in, with people I hoped would become my friends.

At first I felt blessed to be part of more than just a work family. It appeared that many of the store's employees were people of faith. Wendy taught Bible school and Susan led Bible study classes each week in her home.

Once again God has taken care of me and placed me in the perfect setting to learn more about Him.

But working for someone else was quite an adjustment after being self-employed for twenty-three years. I struggled over what felt like being micromanaged and continually spied on. My decisions were constantly questioned.

And I soon learned that the trip I had been so excited to take served a dual purpose: picking diamonds and fine jewelry; and Susan reporting back to the owner about me. She told Wendy that I had been unprofessional by drinking to excess, and that one evening I drank two glasses of wine and three chocolate Martinis.

I was flabbergasted. "What are you talking about?" I told Wendy when she confronted me about that. "There is no truth to that statement."

It soon came out that Susan had been the store's manager before me. Wendy had asked her to step down to sell jewelry and to tend to projects that required her graduate gemologist experience. Apparently, Susan was not happy about it.

I couldn't quit—I'd spent every dollar I had on moving expenses, and my paycheck, along with Tony's Social Security's spousal support, covered my rent and household expenses, but not much else.

What am I going to do?

My experience there only got worse. I felt belittled and disrespected. Every night after work I went home and cried.

Two months into my employment there, I attended a mandatory "Woman of Excellence" meeting. Though the content of the meeting was valuable, I simply didn't want to be there. I certainly wasn't feeling like a woman of excellence.

One of the other attendees noticed that my shoulders were slumped, and instead of mingling with the others, I kept to myself and mostly looked toward the floor. She approached me and stuck her finger in the joint of my back. "You should stand with pride." Her voice was kind but authoritative. "Why are you looking at the floor and not mingling with the other women?" I was not going to share my problems with someone I did not know.

"I can tell from your demeanor that you are troubled about something. My name is Marty L. Ward. I am a transformational strategist. I help people stand up for themselves when they are bullied at school or in the workplace. Would you be open to meeting with me? I know I can help."

Something about her strength and confidence intrigued me. She was definitely a woman of excellence.

"What you need to remember is that you are capable and worthy of living your best life," she said.

I met with Marty in her home a few days later.

"I want you to feel comfortable and know that only good will come from our conversation. Though I am going to ask you questions that may make you uncomfortable, I want you to answer them honestly."

Marty's gift is seeing life's circumstances from a fresh perspective. She takes the sting out of things that are the most difficult to face. While meeting with her, I got the chance to understand the antagonists in my life, like my husband's death, and all that it had revealed afterward was a gift. "It is in knowing yourself that makes the difference between being heard or ignored, feeling empty or empowered."

Three days later, I met with the employees to discuss an upcoming jewelry promotion. I had worked hard to put the promotion in place and felt confident going into the meeting.

But when I arrived, I discovered that Wendy and Susan changed the entire set-up without notifying me.

"Janet, can you please explain to everyone the details of the promotion and how we will be working with clients?"

Immediately I felt there was another set-up going on as well. I took in a deep breath to calm my nerves. "Wendy, apparently you and Susan decided to change the promotion format without notifying me about it. Perhaps it would be best if you explained."

Wendy's face turned from smug to surprised. "Oh," she said, stuttering. "I-I would be happy to."

I smiled within myself. I had stood up to a bully.

That good feeling didn't last. Wendy called me into her office a few weeks later and accused me falsely of mishandling a repair job that cost the company several thousands of dollars—a job that I knew Susan had initiated and handled. Then she fired me.

I knew this was another set-up, so I did not even attempt to defend myself. I simply laughed at the accusations. "Thank you for hiring me. I hope you find your happiness one day."

Wendy's jaw dropped. "I am happy."

I stood and shook my head. "You are not happy. Once you discover your true happiness, you will not need to bully others into making yourself feel good."

In my sessions with Marty, she had taught me to believe in myself so sincerely that nothing a bully could say would steal my confidence. She pointed out that we are only hurt when we believe the bully. But keeping the truth alive inside would allow me not to feel the need to defend myself. I had nothing to defend as I knew the truth of who I was. The bottom line, my boss's words were false. I believed in myself.

Marty helped me see the positive in being fired. She also gave me some great rules to remember and live by:

- I am the only one responsible for my happiness.
- Never allow anyone in my life who causes me pain.
- Walking away requires courage and believing in myself.
- When I feel weak, ask God for help, and He will step in to assist.
- Just because someone says they are a good Christian doesn't mean they are.
- Let them show themselves through their actions and the way they live. If I do not like what I see, I must find my courage and run the other way.

Being unemployed for a little while gave me time to work on myself. I decided this would be an excellent time to visit churches to find my new church family. I also decided that since I had been a business owner for so long, I would try freelancing my jewelry appraisal services.

I made a list of all the jewelers in the area, introduced myself, and started getting some work. That covered some of my expenses, but not enough. I needed a steady paycheck.

Soon after being terminated, an ex-employee contacted me. In the course of our conversation, I found out that Wendy fired forty people in four years. The fired employees formed a club and gathered once a year for drinks. "You're now a member. Would you like to join us for drinks?"

I learned that I was employee #73 at Wendy's jewelry store. Wendy hired Laura, #74 employee, to replace me, but she lasted only four months. She quit because Wendy had bullied her too. Before departing, she secured a job at a local Kay Jewelers.

One day I was in the mall and stopped by the jewelry store. I asked for Laura.

"Hello, my name is Janet Grillo #73."

"I don't understand," Laura said, looking confused. "You are #73?"

"Yes, I was the manager who got fired before Wendy hired you."

Her face immediately changed to understanding, and she smiled. "We should talk. Do you have time for coffee?"

She took her break, and we headed out to the food court where we compared notes and found that Wendy was the biggest bully in town.

"I have a part-time position available," Laura said. "Would you like a job?"

I gladly accepted. After two weeks of working part-time, a full-time employee left. Laura offered me that position, which I again gratefully accepted.

What others meant for harm, God intended for good.

With the job front now secure and settled, I focused on making and building friends. Even though Frankie lived in Orlando, an hour from my house, he visited every other week and stayed a few days each time. We hung out with my family and played a lot of golf. I was glad to hear when Frankie got a girlfriend; our friendship became even more robust. But something concerned me. Every time Frankie visited, I noticed that his steps were becoming slower, and the muscles in his hands weaker. I looked for every opportunity to assist without making him feel helpless.

One of the reasons Frankie liked to visit often was because he fell in love with the scenery and the multitude of birds in my backyard. I usually woke up around 8:00 a.m. only to find that Frankie was enjoying his third cup of coffee, sitting on my porch overlooking the water. I always joined him to enjoy the view.

"I wish I could have a view of the water every day," he said.

"You can," I told him. My stepfather had recently moved from the west coast of Florida to an assisted living home near my sister Diane's house. After Frankie viewed the condominium, he decided that he was going to move there too. His lifelong dream of living near water was coming true.

On August 10, 2015, Frankie, along with his girlfriend, sister, and nephew, drove from Orlando to Melbourne to view Frankie's soon-to-be residence. He secured a home on the eleventh floor of a condominium building overlooking the Banana River. Frankie was so excited and called to share his joy.

"Hey, Juanita, it's Frankie here. I am on my way to Victoria Landing with my relatives and girlfriend. I will call you later. If you get a chance, give me a call. Love you. Bye."

I was working and did not receive the call. I called after work at 9:00 p.m., but he didn't answer.

At 10:00 a.m. the next morning, my phone rang. Caller ID told me it was Frankie.

"Good morning, Frankie! I tried to call—"

"Hello, Janet, this is Aaron, Frankie's nephew. I am calling with sad news. Last night after we returned from Melbourne, Frankie had a heart attack and died."

As he explained the details, my mind shook with disbelief. Finally, I thanked him for calling and letting me know. And I offered assistance if his family needed anything.

When I hung up, I let grief take over. I felt grief over what Frankie had lost. Frankie had only been sixty-eight years old. We'd been looking forward to spending more time together after his move. He would never get to enjoy looking at the boats on the Banana River from his balcony and enjoy visiting the ocean that was only a mile from his new home.

And as for me, I felt grief over losing my best friend.

I remembered how he had confessed feeling terrified about his diagnosis and the quality of life he would soon have to endure. He knew that one day ALS would take over his life. I told him that when the time came, I would open my home to him and gladly assist him in any way possible. Mentally, I had prepared myself for a task that would give him much comfort and love to his dying day. But this unexpected death had robbed us of so much precious time we could have shared.

Frankie had been a spiritual person but not religious. Knowing that his health was declining, though, we'd had many spiritual conversations about God, our spiritual lives, death, and messages from heaven.

A few weeks before he died, I read a story about Harry Houdini. Houdini was a famous escape artist in the early 1900s. He was also exceptionally close to his mother. When she died in the 1920s, his grief was so overwhelming that he began to seek ways to bring her back. He went to numerous mediums and psychics, and he soon learned they were frauds. So upset by this discovery, he became a crusader and focused his energies on debunking them.

He was so devoted to his cause that he made a pact with his wife, Bess, to continue the crusade after he died, to prove once and for all whether Spiritualism was real. He devised a secret code with his wife, Bess—a code only she could verify regarding the message's legitimacy. If no code, then it proved his case.

After he died in 1926 at the age of fifty-two, shortly after receiving an unexpected punch to his abdomen, Bess held seances to contact him every year on the anniversary of his death, October 31, for ten years.

At the end of the final séance, which they held on a rooftop in California, she claimed it was finished. No more seances or attempts to reach her husband. But before everyone exited from the roof, a rainstorm appeared out of a clear sky and drenched the attendees. Then just as suddenly it stopped. One of the attendees, William Larsen said about it:

> To people who do not live in California, this may not seem strange. But California does not have "showers" as do the East and Mid-West. The country is rainless for months. When rain comes, it rains for days. A brief, heavy rain is unheard-of phenomena. Was it a sign? Were the Gods displeased? Was Houdini displeased? Probably it meant nothings for the newspapers failed to mention it. Still, I often wonder.[9]

Another website even mentioned that "as the séance came to an end, a violent storm broke out full of thunder and lightning and drenching everyone involved. The participants would later learn that the storm did not occur anywhere else in the area, only above the séance location."[10]

That sent a chill up my spine! My story about the storm I encountered looking outside my office window in Delaware was the same—how it had come in like a house on fire and exited abruptly without one drop of water on the pavement.

In one of the spiritual conversations that I had with Frankie in the last months of his life, I told him about the Harry Houdini story. We agreed on a message that only the two of us would know. The message was a little out of left field, and it would never be part of a normal conversation. It is a comment that someone made to me when I was in elementary school. (And, of course, I won't share it here, since it's our secret message!)

I will remember many wonderful things about Frankie—our amazing friendship filled with much laughter, our golf outings, and the special love we shared. He was easy to kid around with and rarely got defensive. One time Frankie changed his signature on his email account. And accidentally he typed a lowercase *m* for his middle initial instead of a capital M. From that point on, I greeted him as Francisco Little-m Santiago.

I smiled as I thought about that after his funeral and it brought me great comfort.

In loving memory: Francisco "Frankie" Santiago. December 11, 1947–August 10, 2015

In June 2018, Doug, my ninety-two-year-old stepfather's health took a turn for the worse, and we knew his time on earth was coming to a close. On June 24, Diane and I rushed him to the hospital because he was having stomach issues. While there, he suffered a mini-stroke. He recovered somewhat in a rehabilitation center, but had another stroke complicated with heart issues.

A week later, my family placed him in hospice. For one week, he did not open his eyes, eat, or speak. When I arrived to see him on July 10, I found him lying peacefully in his bed, with his eyes open and unblinking. The trauma of the strokes left his face and body paralyzed. He could not have moved, even if he wanted to.

I sat with him in his room, talking with him about how wonderful his life had been and what a difference he had made in my life for the past forty-five years. I looked at him and saw his face change.

Without warning he displayed a wide "hallelujah-like" smile from ear to ear. It extended from his mouth to his eyes. It reminded me of the Joker's smile from the movie *Batman*. Then he shouted two loud expressions of joy, "Aha! Aha!" And he took his last breath, and died.

It was the most amazing thing I had ever witnessed. He reacted as though he saw Someone in a split second before his death. Perhaps God gave him a glimpse of the spiritual world where he could see God and angels. Perhaps he saw himself as a younger man moving into the next life. His jubilation was so grand to outwardly express himself with so much joy.

Earlier that day, his nephew showed me a photo of Doug when he was in his early twenties. He was Hollywood handsome, and the photo took my breath away. He could have chosen anyone to love. He chose my mother, and I am grateful for that.

After seeing Doug's younger photo, I decided that's how I wanted to remember him. So young and joyful and handsome.

In loving memory: Douglas T. Laning. April 3, 1926–July 10, 2018

Doug served our country as a merchant marine in World War II. After his death, nurses cleansed him and draped his body with an American flag to honor him as a veteran. I said goodbye to him for the final time around 1:00 a.m. when a van arrived to take him to the crematory.

While driving Doug's nephew's wife, Patchie, home, a six-inch frog jumped onto my windshield. It held on for dear life as I drove forty miles per hour down the road. Patchie and I screamed like little girls. When I stopped at a traffic light, I took a picture with my phone.

After a moment, the frog leaped off my car.

Crazy frog, I thought. Then I remembered something, *F-R-O-G means Faithfully Rely On God.*

Doug almost did not make his funeral. The United States Post Office lost the package with his remains. My sister Bobbie waited impatiently at the post office and told the clerk, "The box that you cannot find contains my father's ashes. His funeral service is in two days. I am not leaving until you locate the box."

After two hours, they found the box that contained Doug's ashes. It was stuffed on a shelf behind undeliverable packages.

His funeral service was beautiful. Four members of the military attended, including one who played taps on a trumpet. A representative of our military graced the box of Doug's ashes with an American flag.

After the ceremony, military personnel folded the flag into a triangle and presented it to our family.

How different this funeral was from my husband's. Though I grieved, I was grateful that my stepfather had been blessed to live a full life. There was a calming peace and joy in that.

I had two amazing men in my life—Francisco m. Santiago and Douglas T. Laning—who loved and appreciated me for me. God placed them in my life to grow my confidence and to believe in myself. I'm thankful. And they will forever live in my heart.

No one is actually dead until the ripples they cause in the world die away.
—Terry Pratchett

CHAPTER 15

NEW BEGINNINGS

Life is a journey that must be traveled
no matter how bad the roads and accommodations.
—Oliver Goldsmith

I sat at my dining room table that overlooks the waterway with its beautiful array of birds and sighed contentedly. *I am home. I am at peace.*

After twenty years of moving forward and falling back, of searching for myself and trying to find answers to why things happened the way they did, I am finally in a good place. God has showed Himself over and over to be faithful and kind to me. And I can honestly say, I am content.

At times, the memories of the past flare up, and I cry over what happened and how different life could have been for Tony and me and our marriage. But during those times I soon realize that it does no good to weep over the past. We find our strength in looking forward, in reaching out and helping others, in forgiving.

I did finally complete that rewrite of my book. You hold it now in your hands. As I was working with my editor, going through the revisions and editing process, I looked over it all and became overcome with emotion. I raised my hands in the air and yelled out, "Thank You, God, from the bottom of my heart. I am so grateful for You watching over me and putting amazing people into my life."

My heart felt as though it was going to burst from my chest, it held so much joy. "Alexa, play 'Amazing Grace,'" I said. The notes gently filtered through the air. "Louder, Alexa, louder."

Now the melody rang out as Alan Jackson sang those beautiful words . . .

Amazing Grace! how sweet the sound
That saved a wretch like me!
I once was lost, but now I'm found,
Was blind, but now I see.

'Twas grace that taught my heart to fear,
And grace my fears relieved;
How precious did that grace appear
The hour I first believed!

The Lord hath promised good to me,
His word my hope secures;
He will my shield and portion be
As long as life endures.

When we've been there ten thousand years
Bright shining as the sun,
We've no less days to sing God's praise
Than when we first begun. [11]

I cried listening to every word. It summarized my story perfectly.

I've always loved this song, but now it has a greater meaning. When I was in the midst of the darkest pain, I wasn't sure how, or if, I could come through it. But God walked with me each step of the way.

And as a reminder of where I've been, I have my journals of empowering and comforting quotes and my letters to and from God. Whenever I feel down, I can simply go back to them and find comfort again. And I keep writing, for writing helps us process and document our thoughts, disappointments, wishes, and prayers along the way. They are my proof that God does indeed work amazing things in and for us.

And I know that's true! I was in Mr. Fox's seventh-grade remedial reading class. I was a poor reader and was stereotyped as a slow learner, which made me struggle throughout much of my life with an inferiority complex. I never felt good enough. And now . . . I'm writing books!

So here we are, at the final chapter. Ancient Chinese philosopher Lao Tzu said, "The journey of a thousand miles begins with one step." And I've found that one step leads to the next and to the next, if we keep pressing on.

God has chosen you and me for a specific mission. It is up to us to discover more of ourselves, document our journey, and seek ways to use the lessons that life has taught us along the way. Once we bring God into our plans, great things happen.

We're always going to struggle—that's part of life. Even Jesus said, "In this world, you will have trouble" (John 16:33). Tony Robbins says not to make excuses. If we genuinely want something and are passionate about it, we will find the resources. And we will never give up. With God's help, you and I can move to a place where we are no longer defined by what someone else did. We are no longer defined by who we were. We can learn from those things, forgive, and then position ourselves to fulfill our dreams and purpose. Our purpose doesn't change because someone else made a terrible decision that affected us deeply. Neither do our dreams, though they may morph into something else, something ultimately more beautiful—if we let them. I always remind myself that in God's world, there are no limitations.

Previously when I succeeded on my own, I believed in myself and became relentless in making my dreams come true. When I failed at something, I learned that I did not give my best to succeed or was not resourceful in seeking partners who believed in me, or I simply didn't trust God to be God in my life.

On a bookstore visit, I discovered an excellent book, *Failing Forward: Turning Mistakes Into Stepping Stones for Success* by John C. Maxwell. I am not sure if I found the book on my own or the book found me. But I needed to hear the things he had to say:

- The difference between average people and achieving people is their perception of and their response to failure.
- Wealth is no indicator of high achievement, and poverty is no guarantee of low achievement.
- Many people are training for success when they should be training for failure. Failure is far more common than success; poverty is more prevalent than wealth; disappointment more normal than arrival.
- There is no achievement without failure.

I especially appreciated how he differentiated between failing backward and failing forward:

Failing Backward	**Failing Forward**
Blaming others.	Taking responsibility.
Repeating the same mistakes.	Learning from each mistake.
Expecting never to fail again.	Knowing failure is part of the process.
Expecting to fail continually.	Maintaining a positive attitude.
Thinking I am a failure.	Believing something didn't work.
Quitting.	Persevering.[12]

Reading John Maxwell's book did not permit me to fail; it gave me the wisdom to look at things differently. The bottom line, I am the only person who can label what I do a failure. My jewelry clasp is a prime example. My jeweler and I sat for hours, days, weeks, and months creating and recreating my jewelry clasp.

If we looked at the first production as a failure, the dream of creating the clasp would have died inside of me. However, recreating and rekindling the jewelry clasp with sheer determination to change the face of fashion was an exciting endeavor. After all, no one had created anything similar in more than fifteen years.

I have learned to approach a task or project and give it my very best. No matter what the results, I know that if I am not successful the first time, I will reevaluate the process and try something different. The guarantee of success is never giving up.

As the saying goes, "God uses people who fail—because there aren't any other kind around." No doubt about it, failure is painful. God didn't promise us a lifetime of success. Many times, we believe that we are not good enough. I felt like a failure many times, especially when I lost my home and all of my money, due to the economy and bad business decisions.

However, what I did believe in was myself. I revisited all of my victories. I even went back to the victories I had when I was younger— being a Delaware State Swimming Champion when I was sixteen years old. I held a state record for three years. One year I won a golfing championship at Brandywine Country Club in Wilmington, Delaware. I beat thirty-two women in the challenge. I won the tournament on the last putt on the eighteenth hole.

Each victory builds. One builds on the next and the next and the next. I love how Thomas Edison put it: "I have not failed. I just found 10,000 ways that did not work." Imagine attempting to create a light bulb with naysayers telling you to give up.

Interestingly, many of us think that Thomas Edison invented the light bulb. He did not. Humphry Davy invented the first electric light.

And after him, many men followed, each creating their version and submitting patents. Though Edison was also working on it, he eventually bought the patent rights from two other inventors. Then, in 1879, he invented a carbon filament, which burned for forty hours. This was the prototype we know today as the light bulb.

He didn't give up. But he also learned from others how to succeed. An important lesson.

Jack Canfield and Mark Victor Hansen, coauthors of the *Chicken Soup for the Soul* book series, also understood the importance of failing forward. In the early 1990s, they presented their first book to 145 publishers—and 144 declined. The publishers thought the title was ridiculous and thought a book written about other people's stories would never sell. But one publisher—the 145th—read the stories and decided to give the book a chance. Peter Vegso, publisher of a small health and wellness publishing company in Florida became Chicken Soup for the Soul's founding publisher. Today, that series has sold more than 500 million copies in more than forty languages. It has also launched puzzles and even pet food! All because they didn't give up, no matter the challenges. All because they failed forward.

I read *Failing Forward* at least ten times and carried it like it was my Bible. The book gave me hope to never give up on my dreams. Every time I read a failing forward story, I thought about people in the Bible who never gave up hope, and God granted them miracles. And He is the same today (Hebrews 13:8).

When my husband died, I felt my life slipping away piece by piece. I found hope in the messages of others, such as Joyce Meyer, Tony Robbins, Rhonda Byrne, Joel Osteen, Dr. Robert Schuller, T. D. Jakes, Oprah Winfrey, John Maxwell, Kelly Clarkson, Maria Shriver, and so many more. And I learned to trust and respect the teachers God placed in my life. Teachers such as Monsignor Lemon.

God has placed people in your life too to help guide you and give you hope. If you don't see them there, ask God to show them to you. He will. He can use anyone and anything to encourage and challenge you.

One unlikely source He used was the song "Piece by Piece," written by Kelly Clarkson: "He collected me, up off the ground where you abandoned things." She expressed so well how I felt about what God did for me after Tony's death and secrets. I started my healing from a fetal position. I searched for anything that would get me up off the floor and give me the courage to stand independently. And God provided it through songs, sermons, books, friends, church, and my journals, among so many other things.

During that dark time, I was searching, feeling my way, helpless, not sure what to do or how even to survive. Now that I've pushed through and had my share of failing forward, I've learned a few things, things I know for certain. They are:

- Our God, the God of Light, would not make us go through so much pain without having something beautiful on the other side.
- God works miracles through ordinary events and the people in our lives. He does it through the love and goodwill deeds we do by helping others.
- God is with us 100 percent of the time. Even when He doesn't "feel" present, He is.
- God will not always react to your needs in the way you expect.
- God always responds to your faith.
- The Bible supplies all of our answers to how we should live.

Before Tony's death, even though I attended church with him—because it was the right thing to do—I never made it my own. And I certainly didn't pay all that much attention to the wealth of knowledge and wisdom in the Bible. But after Tony's death, when I began searching, I uncovered that treasure. The Bible teaches us to glorify God, to pray, to give thanks, to be cautious, to help us not conform or give up, and more than I can possibly list here. It's like a roadmap for our lives—guiding us in our relationships, our work, our activities, our marriages, our parenting. And it teaches us the power of faith.

One of my favorite Bible verses is Hebrews 11:3: "By faith we understand that the universe was created by the word of God, so that what is seen was not made out of things that are visible" (esv). It explains faith by combining our sense of the past, present, and future. It confirms that the things hoped for are not seen. The context of the idea tells us that what we have seen and experienced has inspired us to trust God with confidence in the future. Faith is demonstrated by obedience to God, despite a lack of knowledge. We must believe in God for the seed before we can believe in the harvest.

Your dreams must be more significant than what you already have. Let go of the past. Trade your present for the future that you want to have by walking in faith. Trust in God. Choose who you want to believe. The day you decide, the rewards of your life will soon be of greater abundance. And in turn, you, the student, will become the teacher to others who will thirst for change.

I have faith that today will be better than yesterday, and tomorrow will be better than today. That's the hope that God gives us. And He gives because He loves us.

Thinking back over the past sixty-plus years, I know that I have experienced love in many different forms. What I know for sure is the love that I have found in God has been the purest, sweetest, truest. In my past, I often only sought God when I needed help, a shoulder to cry on, or when I was afraid. Today, I think very differently.

I became closer to God in the moments when I was alone, seeking comfort for pain, fear, panic, anxiety, loneliness, disappointment, heartbreak, among many other things. I spent many hours alone and shared my thoughts only with my journal. When I started writing from my heart directly to God, I began to share my joys, pain, and sorrows with Him. He already knew it all, but the beautiful part was that I always felt God was interested in what I was writing.

And slowly with God's help, I began to open myself to be ready to find human love again. I had been so devastated by my husband's death and his wayward life that I was afraid to expose myself to the world of dating. After all, I had not been part of the dating scene for most of my life. I was unsure what I was afraid of—fear of losing? fear of being loved? fear of being hurt? fear of being rejected? Probably all of them at the same time.

A friend encouraged me to find love through the internet, so I chose one and put in my profile. The site matched me with Harrison, a nice, good-looking man who was well educated and had an executive job with the DuPont Company. We had much in common and I enjoyed our company—until he insisted that I pay for 50 percent of everything we did, all of the time. Then we played golf, and I beat him. He didn't take that well.

Our relationship continued and we even went on a vacation together. I did not mind sharing the expenses; however, I would never split a check at the table. I ended the relationship abruptly at the end of our trip, where he presented me with a list of expenses right down to the fifty-cent tolls.

Next, I met a man at the Brandywine Country Club, where I had been a member for eighteen years. We had a great time playing golf. He loved to buy me golf shoes and golf clothes. He was always buying me things—including thirty-three pairs of golf shoes, golf clothes, a high-definition television. And my golf game dramatically improved.

We dated almost a year when I found out that he was a narcissist, pathological liar, drug addict, and drug dealer—with a girlfriend on the side.

Maybe God brought me into his life to make a difference in his life, instead of him making a difference in mine. A fitting way to look for justification in an unjust scenario.

Despite my past love experiences, I am not afraid to love again. I know that when the time is right, God will bring someone into my life. And I will open my heart to a new love and keep my eyes wide open. Most importantly, I will not penalize the possibility of an excellent relationship for failed relationships from my past. Although I will definitely learn as much as possible about the next man before I open my heart to love again.

I was devoted to and in love with my husband. I know that he loved me in the only way he was capable of loving. Writing my story keeps him on my mind always. I know that I can't change the past. Now, I have chosen to remember only the good. I still have a place in my heart touched by my husband's love. I pray that it is in God's plan to fill my heart with a beautiful new love. But for now, I still wait in faith.

And I continue to press forward. I established the nonprofit Journey of Hope Survivors, Inc. to work with those who have been touched by tragedy—whether suicide or post-traumatic stress disorder (PTSD) from returning from war. Many people feel hopeless in what appears to be desperate situations—but there is always hope.

I created a board of directors with outstanding qualifications in global leadership, social services, business, and digital marketing. Together my plan is to create centers throughout the world to educate, encourage, inspire, and help people find a new purpose for their lives after they have faced a tragedy. Our goal is to help transform victims to victory.[13]

I also started a podcast, *Victims to Victory,* which features interviews with doctors, suicide activists, influencers, and more. After I first self-published this book in 2018, I had the opportunity to attend a National Publicity Summit in New York City. During the event, I met with representatives from magazines, radio, podcasts, and television, including Tami Devine, co-owner of Crown City News in Pasadena, California.

We spoke about how we could work together to help bring awareness to veteran suicides, which are on the rise. I often wondered why two people who returned from war with a similar injury, possibly losing both legs, would have a different recovery. One would recover by strapping on prosthetic legs and run a marathon, while the other would become a martyr, an alcoholic, a drug addict, and eventually commit suicide.

I truly believe the difference is one turning to God for help and understanding. God chooses the weak to become healthy by overcoming the adversities in our lives. We are more credible witnesses, and others with similar challenges can relate to us.

One of my assignments with Tami was to interview veterans whose lives were touched by suicide. My first interview was with a man named Ricardo "Rich" Alvarez Jr. Rich suffered from PTSD and found himself unemployed living in a box. He attempted to commit suicide three times until he realized that he wanted to live and not die. Today, Rich is a motivational speaker and owns a computer repair business.

I interviewed a Gold Star mom whose son committed suicide after suffering from PTSD. His family helped him to the best of their ability. He died after his fourth attempt. The mother introduced me to a man named Howard M. Berry, Jr. His son, Staff Sergeant Joshua Berry, had PTSD and committed suicide in 2013.

Howard was a champion who brought national attention to veteran suicides. He started a demonstration of 660 flags to represent the 660 veteran suicide deaths in one month. While talking with my sister Billie about the flags, she commented that she had seen an extensive collection of American flags gathered together but never knew what they meant.

Hearing so many of these stories, I felt strongly that I needed to *do* something to help shed some light on what our veterans and their families are going through. On average, 22 American veterans commit suicide every day; 660 each month; and more than 7,000 every year. I got to work and designed the *Veterans Suicide Awareness flag*.

There are 50 stars total on the flag. Thirty of the stars are a combination of white and turquoise. Each of those 30 stars have the number 22 displayed on them in either purple or white. Thirty times 22 equals 660—the number of veteran suicides each month. The flag also has two turquoise stripes. Turquoise and purple are the designated colors for suicide prevention.

In between in two turquoise stripes reads, "Stop 22 Veteran Suicides a Day." (You can view the flag at www.veteranssuicideawareness.org.)

Ideally, I'd love to see communities and businesses sponsor these flags and donate them to veteran locations—such as VA medical Centers, community-based outpatient clinics, Veterans Benefits Administrations, and national cemeteries—to fly beneath the American flag.

As you and I both know only too well, PTSD is not exclusive to veterans. Anyone who has suffered from trauma can have PTSD. Anyone who has lost a loved one to suicide will more than likely have symptoms of PTSD.

When I was seeking ways to help make a difference in veterans' lives, I found the *Dare to Care Mental Health Life Coaching Program.* It is an online course sponsored by Light University in Forest, Virginia. They are the leader in certificate and diploma-based Christian counseling education. I chose to take the courses to understand better the audiences that I want to reach. Education and empathy are the keys to understanding. We all need to have a better grasp of the problem before we can help with the solution.[14]

I planned to call Howard Berry and tell him about the Veterans Suicide Awareness flag and my quest to join his mission to bring awareness to veteran suicides. But I was too late. Howard died on June 17, 2020. I know he would have loved the flag and what it stands for. As crazy as it sounds, I believe that the day Howard died was a message from God for me to continue with Howard's quest. I was born on June 17, 1949. He died on my birthday.

One day I received a phone call out of the blue from Tony Stephan of Renova Worldwide. Tony heard that I was working with veterans with PTSD.

"My wife, Debbie, had a hard-fought battle with mental illness. In 1994 she committed suicide, leaving our nine children and me behind. Several of my children suffered from mental health issues as well. Healthcare professionals told me that it was probable that one of my children would likely suffer the same fate as their mother due to the severity of his symptoms. They offered little hope."

"I'm so sorry," I told him.

"I was desperate and knew that I had to find a way to save the lives of my children," he continued. "I learned about micronutrient formulations used for livestock and began experimenting with combinations for my afflicted children. In 1996, I gave the developed nutrient formula to two of my kids. Both responded quickly and experienced an increase in calm, coping, and mental clarity."

"That's wonderful," I said, though unsure why he was telling me this.

"In 2018, we developed a product called Empower Plus. The EMP Lightning Stik package is like an individual serving of Crystal Light. The user puts the product under their tongue, and it dissolves instantly. Within moments users experience a calm and clarity."

He encouraged me to go to YouTube and hear a testimony from Tristian Custer. He was a drug addict with depression and suicidal thoughts, who experienced incredible results after taking the product for eleven days.

"If this is something that can help others who are struggling with suicidal thoughts, maybe you would be interested in helping get the word out?" he said.

I listened and promised to check out the video and do some research before I made any decision. I did, and I was impressed. Today, Renova Worldwide is one of my sponsors.[15] They support me with product that enables me to share with others to experience the amazing calming effects of their Empower Plus products.

When I look back at everything that has happened since Tony's death, I am amazed at the doors God has opened for me and given me the strength to walk through. Businesses started, jewelry clasp and flags created, and most important, people touched and helped. Who says we have to "be somebody" in order to do something life-changing for others?

You and I may never be a Mother Teresa or Thomas Edison or Oprah Winfrey. That's okay. We aren't supposed to be those people. God made us *us*, not them. And He created us, knowing that one day, we would suffer tragedy. And He wants to heal and use our past for a brighter future for us and for others.

You already have what it takes to help make our world a better place. Making a difference in the world may seem like an enormous task—especially if you're still in the throes of despair and need someone to help you—but I've found that helping others brings healing and comfort when we least expect it and most need it. Reach out. The size of the contribution is not what matters most. The key is to have the heart to do it. As Anne Frank said, "How wonderful it is that nobody needs to wait a single moment before starting to improve the world."

There is no one best time to start to make a difference in the world. You don't need to wait till you have the time to share some love; you don't have to wait till you make more money to share a slice of bread. Little efforts count, and you can start making small contributions today.

If you think that everything has been taken care of by somebody and your contribution is not going to make much of a difference, then you're wrong. If you think you're too broken and have nothing to offer somebody else in need, you're wrong. You have a purpose. Tragedy doesn't change that. God wants to use you to bring you healing and to bring healing to others!

As the saying goes, "To receive, you must first give." The more you give, the more you'll receive.

You can change the world by helping one person at a time. One of the ways to help someone is to empower a person. But how do you empower a person? Well, one of the ways is to be generous in giving praise and encouragement instead of criticism.

By praising and encouraging someone, you actually help him or her to accomplish what that person is meant to be. And that leads to more value being added to the world.

Benjamin Disraeli once said, "The greatest good you can do for another is not just to share your riches, but to reveal to him his own."

It's his version of "Give a man a fish, you feed him for a day. Teach him how to fish, you feed him for a lifetime.'

The good that we seek to do *will* make a difference.

In addition to doing things to make a difference, we should also seek to influence others to start doing things that make a difference. And the best way to convince other people is to lead by example. Start where you are and start showing more concern and love to the people around you. Start to make monthly donations to your favorite charity. Start putting more effort in your work to increase the value output.

Every effort counts, no matter how small and insignificant it may seem. Just do something and do something good. You will be glad that you did. And soon you will find yourself no long dwelling so much in the pain of the past.

Brian Vaczily said, "Falling down is how we grow. Staying down is how we die." It's true. I created my own quote that is a bit similar:

> When you stop dreaming about your future, you die. First,
> you die on the inside, and then you die on the outside.

It reminds me of a story I experienced. On May 31, 2009, I prepared myself to enter a 5K run/walk in honor of a friend who died from a blood clot. Mike Clark mastered three Ironman Triathlons and worked as a critical player in the Boys and Girls Club in Wilmington, Delaware. Kids were his life.

After the race began, I noticed a young boy struggling to run back to the starting line. He had been running with his team, the Fast Cats—he was wearing a Fast Cats T-shirt—but now he had a worried look on his face.

"Do you need help?" I asked.

Through extreme difficulty breathing, he replied, "I'm having an asthma attack and I do not have my inhaler. My mother has it, but I do not know where to find her."

"Come with me to my car," I said, without hesitation. "I have an inhaler that you can use."

On our walk to my car, I found out his name was Xavier and he was twelve years old.

I had experienced many asthma attacks both as a child and as an adult and knew how Xavier felt. The farther we walked, the more he began to cry. His airway was swelling, causing shortness of breath, and he was wheezing. He was holding onto his chest, gasping for air. I knew he was frightened.

"Calm down, Xavier, I can see my car from here. You can use my inhaler and take it with you. I will also give you a bottle of water."

A few minutes after he used the inhaler, his tears dried up and his face turned happy. "I'm feeling better. Thank you for helping me."

"Let's find a way to rejoin the race," I said.

My first mission was to find my eight-year-old granddaughter, who ran many yards in front of me after the race began. Xavier and I discovered a shortcut and started to look for Mackenzie. All the runners passed, and I could not find her. "Xavier, please sit on a bench while I search for my granddaughter. I will be back shortly."

I discovered that Mackenzie was the last person in the race, slowly walking with no runners in sight.

As soon as she saw me, her face showed relief. "Mom-Mom, where did you go? I looked for you after the race began and I could not find you. I decided to walk, hoping you would catch up to me."

"When I was running, I met a young boy who was having an asthma attack. I walked him to my car to get my inhaler. Are you okay? Were you scared?"

"No," she said. "I saw the markings on the road, and I followed the path."

I was proud of her.

We joined Xavier, and the three of us walked together for about a mile. My daughter, who finished second in the race, ran back to find us.

"Mom, are you okay? What is taking you so long to finish the race?" she asked.

I explained what had happened.

Satisfied, she announced that she was going to run another mile to cool down. "I'll come back to join you."

When she returned, she was running with Vicki Huber-Rudawsky. Vicki was the winner of the race. She is also a twice Olympian runner.

We all began to walk the last mile together when I had a beautiful thought. "Vicki, would you run with Xavier?" I said. "That way, he can tell his friends that he ran with an Olympian runner."

"It would be my pleasure!" Vicki replied.

We all began to run until I realized that I could not keep up with the pace. Vicki turned to see me slowing down and motioned to walk with us instead of running.

"That's okay," I said, waving them on. "You run with Xavier."

They took off at an incredible pace. Although I could not see his face, I knew that Xavier was grinning from ear to ear. An asthma attack was not part of God's plan at this time.

Vicki and Xavier ran to the finish line together. His entire team, The Fast Cats, were there to cheer him across the end. Xavier began his race as a disabled child with fear and gasping for his breath. He completed his run with help, hope, vision, enthusiasm, and a fantastic victory that no one could have imagined. God loves receiving credit for seemingly impossible situations.

I commended Vicki for being a role model for this twelve-year-old boy and his teammates. She made a simple but profound difference in the lives of those children.

We are all children of God, no matter what our age. Unfortunately, many children have lost their way. There is no promise of tomorrow in the Bible. We must treat each day as a gift from God and cherish every moment.

When my granddaughter, Mackenzie, was four-years-old, she asked,

"Mom-Mom, do you know that I have special powers? I wish that I was nocturnal because then I could see in the dark." I wasn't sure why she wished that she was nocturnal. I would think that seeing in the dark would be part of her special powers. However, to a four-year-old, it made perfect sense.

"No, I did not know that you have special powers," I said, looking most impressed at her. "Where can I get some?"

"All you have to do is ask God, and He will give them to you," she said, smiling brightly.

Today, Mackenzie is twenty years old. At the age of four, she knew that she had special powers. She also had a thirst for a clearer vision so that she could see in the dark.

As we get closer to God, we will begin to remove ourselves from the darkness. We will discover that God's light and powers are within all of us. It is our job to find out what is already there. I am amazed that such wisdom came from a four-year-old.

When all of God's children understand that we are not alone and discover that we are the only ones who can embrace our special powers—special healing powers that don't disappear when tragedy and pain enter our lives, we will be changed, healed, empowered. And in turn, we will use those special healing powers to make a difference in the lives of others.

God promised me wings to fly. He promised you wings to fly as well. There is hope for surviving suicide. And not just surviving, but truly thriving and making the world a better place—not in spite of the tragedy, but because of it.

In gratitude and joy,

Janet V. Grillo

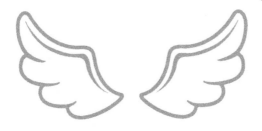

A Place to Grieve and Heal

As you've read through my story, even though it will be different from your own, I hope that something resonated with you. As you think back over these pages and what I discovered, perhaps you'd like to take some time to write down your thoughts about what might be helpful for you to remember in your own healing. On the next few pages, you'll find space to do so—or at least to get you started. I'd recommend that you also purchase a journal to keep track of your own healing journey.

_____

_____

_____

_____

_____

_____

More from Janet V. Grillo

Check out Janet's second book, *My Victory Journal*. It's a self-help journal, to be published in 2022. In it, Janet guides you to take a closer look at your life, find answers to what bothers you, and it will help you find your true passion and purpose. Once you acknowledge what God is directing you to do in your life, the journal writing prompts will help you begin to see your trials and disappointments as stepping stones to becoming a better person.

Sprinkled through are positive quotations and passages from the Bible, along with writing prompts to write directly to God. You can write from your heart straight to God, and yes, sometimes, God will write back to you. In addition, Janet shares with you the profound wisdom she discovered along the way on her journey.

For more information about this and other books, jewelry, and events, go to www.janetgrilloauthor.com.

ABOUT THE AUTHOR

Janet V. Grillo believes in new beginnings. After her husband died of a self-inflicted gunshot wound, Janet had to pick up the pieces of her shattered life, embrace her faith, and learn how to live again. Now a suicide advocate, she finds comfort, peace, and joy in helping others who have also experienced the ravages of suicide in a family or friend's life. She is the founder of the nonprofit Journey of Hope Survivors Inc., an organization that helps those who have suffered a tragedy. She also hosts the podcast *Victims to Victory*, in which she interviews doctors, suicide activists, and influencers, as well as others. For information about the podcasts and weekly meetings in your city, visit www.victimstovictory.support. The CEO of Veterans Suicide Awareness, Janet is also the creator of the Veterans Suicide Awareness flag, which has received national attention. A Wilmington, Delaware, native, she moved to Viera, Florida, in 2014 and now calls that home. She has four sisters, a daughter, and one granddaughter. To find out more, to sign up for her updates on speaking engagements or book releases, or to connect with Janet, visit her at www.janetgrilloauthor.com.

Renova Worldwide

- EMP Lightening Stiks – The most important nutritional supplement in the world.
- The nutrients in EmPowerplus helps promote a healthier and balanced lifestyle.
- 34+ Independent medical research studies.
- 30 million dollars. Spent in independent research.
- Promotes calmness, clarity and focus.
- Alleviates stress, increases energy and boosts the immune system.
- Canadian company – 23+ years of testimonies and success.
- www.journeyofhope.renovaworldwide.com

NOTES

1   Howard Bronson and Mike Riley, *How to Heal a Broken Heart in 30 Days: A Day-by-Day Guide to Saying Good-bye and Getting on with Your Life* (New York: Broadway), 2002. Excerpt used by permission of the authors. All rights reserved.

2   For more information about the jewelry or to order, go to www.janetvgrillo.com and enter your email address to be added to my database. I will notify you when the clasp and necklaces are available.

3   Ainz, "Diamond in the Rough," Urban Dictionary, January 24, 2006, https://www.urbandictionary.com/define.php?term=Diamond%20in%20the%20rough.

4   Naomi Long Madgett, "Woman with Flower," in *Star by Star*, 1965. Used by permission.

5   Rhonda Byrne, *The Secret* (New York: Atria Books, 2006, 2108), 116.

6   Byrne, *The Secret*, 117.

7   "Viera," Wikipedia, accessed February 23, 2021, https://en.wikipedia.org/wiki/Viera.

8   "The Swan Spirit Animal," Spirit Animal, accessed February 23, 2021, https://www.spiritanimal.info/swan-spirit-animal/.

9   John Cox, "Halloween 1936: The Final Houdini Séance," Wild About Harry, October 31, 2014, https://www.wildabouthoudini. com/2014/10/halloween-1936-final-houdini-seance.html.

10 "Houdini and the Supernatural," The Great Harry Houdini, accessed February 25, 2021, https://www.thegreatharryhoudini. com/occult.html.

11 John Newton, "Amazing Grace," 1772, public domain.

12 John C. Maxwell, *Failing Forward* (Nashville: Thomas Nelson, 2000).

13 For more information, go to www.journeyofhopesurvivors.org.

14 If you are interested in knowing more about this program, email info@veteranssuicideawareness.org.

15 To learn more, go to www.journeyofhope.renovaworldwide.com and janet@journeyofhopesurvivors.org.

A free ebook edition is available with the purchase of this book.

To claim your free ebook edition:

1. Visit MorganJamesBOGO.com
2. Sign your name CLEARLY in the space
3. Complete the form and submit a photo of the entire copyright page
4. You or your friend can download the ebook to your preferred device

Morgan James BOGO™

A **FREE** ebook edition is available for you or a friend with the purchase of this print book.

CLEARLY SIGN YOUR NAME ABOVE

Instructions to claim your free ebook edition:
1. Visit MorganJamesBOGO.com
2. Sign your name CLEARLY in the space above
3. Complete the form and submit a photo of this entire page
4. You or your friend can download the ebook to your preferred device

Print & Digital Together Forever.

Snap a photo   Free ebook   Read anywhere